The Book of Revelation is a work of profound theology. But its literary form makes it impenetrable to many modern readers and open to all kinds of misinterpretations. Richard Bauckham explains how the book's imagery conveyed meaning in its original context and how the book's theology is inseparable from its literary structure and composition. Revelation is seen to offer not an esoteric and encoded forecast of historical events but rather a theocentric vision of the coming of God's universal kingdom, contextualized in the late first-century world dominated by Roman power and ideology. It calls on Christians to confront the political idolatries of the time and to participate in God's purpose of gathering all the nations into his kingdom. Once Revelation is properly grounded in its original context it is seen to transcend that context and speak to the contemporary church. This study concludes by highlighting Revelation's continuing relevance for today.

NEW TESTAMENT THEOLOGY

General Editor: James D. G. Dunn,
Lightfoot Professor of Divinity, University of Durham

The theology of the Book of Revelation

This series provides a programmatic survey of the individual writings of the New Testament. It aims to remedy the deficiency of available published material, which has tended to concentrate on historical, textual, grammatical and literary issues at the expense of the theology, or to lose distinctive emphases of individual writings in systematized studies of 'The Theology of Paul' and the like. New Testament specialists here write at greater length than is usually possible in the introductions to commentaries or as part of other New Testament theologies, and explore the theological themes and issues of their chosen books without being tied to a commentary format, or to a thematic structure drawn from elsewhere. When complete, the series will cover all the New Testament writings, and will thus provide an attractive, and timely, range of texts around which courses can be developed.

THE THEOLOGY OF THE BOOK OF REVELATION

RICHARD BAUCKHAM

Professor of New Testament Studies
St Mary's College, University of St Andrews

CAMBRIDGE
UNIVERSITY PRESS

CAMBRIDGE
UNIVERSITY PRESS

University Printing House, Cambridge CB2 8BS, United Kingdom

Cambridge University Press is part of the University of Cambridge.

It furthers the University's mission by disseminating knowledge in the pursuit of education, learning and research at the highest international levels of excellence.

www.cambridge.org
Information on this title: www.cambridge.org/9780521356916

First published 1993
30th printing 2019

Printed in the United Kingdom by TJ International Ltd. Padstow, Cornwall

A catalogue record for this publication is available from the British Library

Library of Congress Cataloguing in Publication data
Bauckham, Richard.
The theology of the Book of Revelation / Richard Bauckham.
p. cm. – (New Testament theology)
Includes bibliographical references
ISBN 0 521 35610 5 (hardback) – ISBN 0 521 35691 1 (paperback)
1. Bible, N.T. Revelation – Theology. I. Title. II. Series.
BS2825.2B387 1993
228'.06–dc 20   92-15805 CIP

ISBN 978-0-521-35691-6 Paperback

For Loveday and Philip Alexander

Contents

Editor's preface

Although the New Testament is usually taught within Departments or Schools or Faculties of Theology/Divinity/Religion, theological study of the individual New Testament writings is often minimal or at best patchy. The reasons for this are not hard to discern.

For one thing, the traditional style of studying a New Testament document is by means of straight exegesis, often verse by verse. Theological concerns jostle with interesting historical, textual, grammatical and literary issues, often at the cost of the theological. Such exegesis is usually very time-consuming, so that only one or two key writings can be treated in any depth within a crowded three-year syllabus.

For another, there is a marked lack of suitable textbooks round which courses could be developed. Commentaries are likely to lose theological comment within a mass of other detail in the same way as exegetical lectures. The section on the theology of a document in the Introduction to a commentary is often very brief and may do little more than pick out elements within the writing under a sequence of headings drawn from systematic theology. Excursuses usually deal with only one or two selected topics. Likewise larger works on New Testament Theology usually treat Paul's letters as a whole and, having devoted the great bulk of their space to Jesus, Paul and John, can spare only a few pages for others.

In consequence, there is little incentive on the part of teacher or student to engage with a particular New Testament document, and students have to be content with a general overview, at best complemented by in-depth study of (parts of) two or three New Testament writings. A serious corollary to this is the degree to which students are thereby incapacitated in the task of integrating their New Testament study with the rest of their Theology or Religion courses, since often they are capable only of drawing on the general overview or on a sequence of particular verses treated atomistically. The growing importance of a literary-critical approach to individual documents simply highlights the present deficiencies even more. Having been given little experience in handling individual New Testament writings as such at a theological level, most students are very ill-prepared to develop a properly integrated literary and theological response to particular texts. Ordinands too need more help than they currently receive from textbooks, so that their preaching from particular passages may be better informed theologically.

There is need therefore for a series to bridge the gap between too brief an introduction and too full a commentary where theological discussion is lost among too many other concerns. It is our aim to provide such a series. That is, a series where New Testament specialists are able to write at greater length on the theology of individual writings than is usually possible in the introductions to commentaries or as part of New Testament Theologies, and to explore the theological themes and issues of these writings without being tied to a commentary format or to a thematic structure provided from elsewhere. The volumes seek both to describe each document's theology, and to engage theologically with it, noting also its canonical context and any specific influence it may have had on the history of Christian faith and life. They are directed at those who already have one or two years of full-time New Testament and theological study behind them.

James D. G. Dunn
University of Durham

Abbreviations

Isa.	Isaiah
Jer.	Jeremiah
Josephus, *Ant.*	Josephus, *Antiquitates Judaicae*
Jos. As.	Joseph and Asenath
Jub.	Jubilees
Judg.	Judges
L.A.B.	Pseudo-Philo, *Liber Antiquitatum Biblicarum*
Lad. Jac.	Ladder of Jacob
Liv. Proph.	Lives of the Prophets
Matt.	Matthew
Mic.	Micah
Num.	Numbers
Odes Sol.	Odes of Solomon
1 Pet.	1 Peter
2 Pet.	2 Peter
Philo, *Mos.*	Philo, *De Vita Mosis*
Philo, *Plant.*	Philo, *De Plantatione*
Ps.	Psalm
1QGen.Apoc.	Genesis Apocryphon from Qumran Cave 1
1QH	Hodayot (Thanksgiving Hymns) from Qumran Cave 1
1QM	Milhamah (War Scroll) from Qumran Cave 1
4QpIsa.	Pesher on Isaiah from Qumran Cave 4
1QSb	Blessings from Qumran Cave 1
Rev.	Revelation
Rom.	Romans
1 Sam.	1 Samuel
2 Sam.	2 Samuel
Sir.	Ben Sira (Ecclesiasticus)
2 Tim.	2 Timothy
T.Levi	Testament of Levi
Tob.	Tobit
Zech.	Zechariah

Serial publications

AARSR	American Academy of Religion Studies on Religion

BETL	Bibliotheca Ephemeridum Theologicarum Lovaniensium
BNTC	Black's New Testament Commentaries
BZNW	Beihefte zur *Zeitschrift für die neutestamentliche Wissenschaft*
EQ	*Evangelical Quarterly*
Int.	*Interpretation*
JBL	*Journal of Biblical Literature*
JSNTSS	*Journal for the Study of the New Testament* Supplement Series
JSOTSS	*Journal for the Study of the Old Testament* Supplement Series
NCB	New Century Bible
Neot.	*Neotestamentica*
NTS	*New Testament Studies*
RTP	*Revue de Théologie et de Philosophie*
SNTSMS	SNTS Monograph Series
TDNT	G. Kittel, ed., *Theological Dictionary of the New Testament*, 10 vols. (trans. G. W. Bromiley; Grand Rapids: Eerdmans, 1964–76)
Them.	*Themelios*
TU	Texte und Untersuchungen
TynB	*Tyndale Bulletin*
WUNT	Wissenschaftliche Untersuchungen zum Neuen Testament
ZNW	*Zeitschrift für die neutestamentliche Wissenschaft*

CHAPTER I

Reading the Book of Revelation

WHAT KIND OF A BOOK IS REVELATION?

It is important to begin by asking this question, because our answer determines our expectations of the book, the kind of meaning we expect to find in it. One of the problems readers of the New Testament have with Revelation is that it seems an anomaly among the other New Testament books. They do not know how to read it. Misinterpretations of Revelation often begin by misconceiving the kind of book it is.

At least in the case of ancient books, the beginning of the work is usually the essential indication of the kind of book it is intended to be. The opening verses of Revelation seem to indicate that it belongs not to just one but to three kinds of literature. The first verse, which is virtually a title, speaks of the *revelation* of Jesus Christ, which God gave him and which reaches God's servants through a chain of revelation: God → Christ → angel → John (the writer) → the servants of God. The word 'revelation' or 'apocalypse' (*apokalypsis*) suggests that the book belongs to the genre of ancient Jewish and Christian literature which modern scholars call apocalypses, and even though we cannot in fact be sure that the word itself already had this technical sense when John used it there is a great deal in Revelation which resembles the other works we call apocalypses.

However, 1:3 describes Revelation as a *prophecy* intended to be read aloud in the context of Christian worship, and this claim to be a prophecy is confirmed by the epilogue to the book (cf. 22:6–7, which echoes 1:1–3, and especially 22:18–19). But

I

then 1:4–6 can leave no doubt that Revelation is intended to be a *letter*. Verses 4–5a follow the conventional form of letter-opening used by Paul and other early Christian leaders: statement of writer and addressees, followed by a greeting in the form: 'Grace to you and peace from . . .' There are differences from Paul's usual form, but the early Christian letter form is clear and is confirmed by the conclusion of the book (22:21), which is comparable with the conclusions of many of Paul's letters. Thus Revelation seems to be an apocalyptic prophecy in the form of a circular letter to seven churches in the Roman province of Asia. This is explicit in 1:11: what is revealed to John (what he 'sees') he is to write and send to the seven churches which are here named. This command applies to all the visions and revelations which follow in the rest of the book. The habit of referring to chapters 2–3 as the seven 'letters' to the churches is misleading. These are not as such letters but prophetic messages to each church. It is really the whole book of Revelation which is one circular letter to the seven churches. The seven messages addressed individually to each church are introductions to the rest of the book which is addressed to all seven churches. Thus we must try to do justice to the three categories of literature – apocalypse, prophecy and letter – into which Revelation seems to fall. In considering each in turn it will be appropriate to begin with prophecy.

REVELATION AS CHRISTIAN PROPHECY

Virtually all we know about John, the author of Revelation, is that he was a Jewish Christian prophet. Evidently he was one of a circle of prophets in the churches of the province of Asia (22:6), and evidently he had at least one rival: the Thyatiran prophetess whom he considers a false prophet (2:20). Thus to understand his book we must situate it in the context of early Christian prophecy. John must normally have been active as a prophet in the churches to which he writes. The seven messages to the churches reveal detailed knowledge of each local situation, and 2:21 presumably refers to an earlier prophetic oracle of his, addressed to the prophetess he calls Jezebel at Thyatira.

John was no stranger to these churches but had exercised a prophetic ministry in them and knew them well.

Since Christian prophets normally prophesied in the context of Christian worship meetings, we must assume that this is what John usually did. The reading of this written prophecy in the worship service (1:3) was therefore a substitute for John's more usual presence and prophesying in person. Usually in the early churches prophets delivered oracles which were given to them by God in the worship meeting. They declared the revelation as they received it (cf. 1 Cor. 14:30; Hermas, *Mand.* 11:9). It took the form of a word of God spoken to the church, under the inspiration of the Spirit, in the name of God or the risen Christ, so that the 'I' of the oracle was the divine person addressing the church through the prophet (cf. Odes Sol. 42:6). But early Christian prophets seem also to have received visionary revelations which they conveyed to the church later in the form of a report of the vision (cf. Acts 10:9–11:18; Hermas, *Vis.* 1–4). In this case the vision was initially a private experience, even if it happened during the worship service, and was only subsequently reported to the church as prophecy. We can make a useful, though not absolute, distinction between these two types of prophecy: oracles, spoken in the name of God or Christ, and reports of visions, in which the prophets had received revelations in order subsequently to pass them on to others. The whole book of Revelation is a report of visionary revelation, but it also includes oracular prophecy within it. This occurs in the prologue (1:8) and the epilogue (22:12–13, 16, 20); the seven messages to the churches (2:1–3:22) are oracles written as Christ's word to the churches; and also throughout the book (e.g. 13:9–10; 14:13b; 16:15) there are prophetic oracles which interrupt the accounts of the visions.

Yet if Revelation resembles in a very general way the kind of prophecy John might have delivered orally in person, it is also a far more elaborate and studied composition than any extemporary prophecy could have been. Revelation is a literary work composed with astonishing care and skill. We should certainly not doubt that John had remarkable visionary experiences, but he has transmuted them through what must have been a lengthy process of reflection and writing into a thoroughly literary creation which is designed not to reproduce the experience so much as to communicate the meaning of the revelation that had been given him. Certainly Revelation is a literary work designed for oral performance (1:3), but as a complex literary creation, dense with meaning and allusion, it must be qualitatively different from the spontaneous orality of most early Christian prophecy.

Therefore it may not have been just because he could not be with his churches in person that he wrote this prophecy. He wrote from Patmos (1:9), an inhabited island not far from Ephesus. It has most often been assumed that 1:9 indicates he was exiled there, whether in flight from persecution or legally banished to the island. This is possible, but it is also possible that he went to Patmos in order to receive the revelation ('on account of the word of God and the testimony of Jesus' could refer back to 1:2, where these terms describe what he 'saw'; but on the other hand, cf. 6:9; 20:4).

Although most early Christian prophecy was oral, not written, John had plenty of models for a written prophecy, both in the prophetic books of the Hebrew scriptures and in the later Jewish apocalypses. In its literary forms what he writes is indebted to both kinds of model. It is clear that John saw himself, not only as one of the Christian prophets, but also as standing in the tradition of Old Testament prophecy. For example, in 10:7 he hears that 'the mystery of God will be fulfilled, as he announced to his servants the prophets'. The reference (with allusion to Amos 3:7) is almost certainly to the Old Testament prophets. But then John goes on to record his own prophetic commissioning (10:8–11) in a form which is modelled on that of Ezekiel (Ezek. 2:9–3:3). His task is to proclaim the fulfilment of what God had revealed to the prophets of the past. The whole book is saturated with allusions to Old Testament prophecy, though there are no formal quotations. As a prophet himself, John need not quote his predecessors, but he takes up and reinterprets their prophecies, much as the later writers in the Old Testament prophetic tradition themselves took up and reinterpreted earlier prophecies. It is a remarkable fact, for example, that John's great oracle against Babylon (18:1–19:8) echoes every one of the oracles against Babylon in the Old Testament prophets, as well as the two major oracles against Tyre.[1] It seems that John not only writes in the tradition of the Old Testament prophets, but understands himself to be writing at the climax of the tradition, when all the eschatological oracles of the prophets are about to be finally fulfilled, and so he interprets and gathers them up in his own prophetic revelation. What makes him a Christian prophet is that he does so in the light of the fulfilment already of Old Testament prophetic expectation in the victory of the Lamb, the Messiah Jesus.

REVELATION AS AN APOCALYPSE

Biblical scholarship has long distinguished between Old Testament prophecy and the Jewish apocalypses, which include the Old Testament book of Daniel as well as such extra-canonical works as 1 Enoch, 4 Ezra and 2 Baruch. The extent and character of the continuity and the differences between prophecy and apocalyptic are highly debatable. But the distinction means that the relationship between Revelation and the Jewish apocalypses has also been debated. Often the issue has been posed in a misleading way, as though John himself would have made the kinds of distinction modern scholars have made between prophecy and apocalyptic. This is very unlikely. The book of Daniel, which was one of John's major Old Testament sources, he would certainly have regarded as a prophetic book. If he knew some of the post-biblical apocalypses, as he most probably did, he will have seen them as a form of prophecy. The forms and traditions which Revelation shares with other works we call apocalypses John will have used as vehicles of prophecy, in continuity with Old Testament prophecy.

We may still ask in what sense Revelation belongs to the

---

[1] Babylon: Isa. 13:1–14:23; 21:1–10; 47; Jer 25:12–38; 50–1. Tyre: Isa. 23; Ezek. 26–28. For this point, as with many other aspects of Revelation's use of the Old Testament, I am indebted to the important work of J. Fekkes III, 'Isaiah and Prophetic Traditions in the Book of Revelation: Visionary Antecedents and their Development' (Ph.D. thesis, University of Manchester, 1988).

genre of ancient religious literature we call the apocalypse. J. J. Collins defines the literary genre apocalypse in this way:

'Apocalypse' is a genre of revelatory literature with a narrative framework, in which a revelation is mediated by an otherworldly being to a human recipient, disclosing a transcendent reality which is both temporal, insofar as it envisages eschatological salvation, and spatial, insofar as it involves another, supernatural world.[2]

The reference to eschatological salvation would be disputed in some recent study of the apocalypses. Although the apocalypses have conventionally been thought to be about history and eschatology, this is not necessarily true of all of them. The heavenly secrets revealed to the seer in the extant Jewish apocalypses cover a rather wide range of topics and are not exclusively concerned with history and eschatology.[3] John's apocalypse, however, is exclusively concerned with eschatology: with eschatological judgment and salvation, and with the impact of these on the present situation in which he writes. The heavenly revelation he receives concerns God's activity in history to achieve his eschatological purpose for the world. In other words, John's concerns are exclusively prophetic. He uses the apocalyptic genre as a vehicle of prophecy, as not all Jewish apocalyptists did consistently. So it would be best to call John's work a prophetic apocalypse or apocalyptic prophecy. With that qualification, it obviously fits the definition of the genre apocalypse quoted above, and there should be no difficulty in recognizing its generic relationship to the Jewish apocalypses, while at the same time acknowledging its continuity with Old Testament prophecy.

There are many ways in which John's work belongs to the apocalyptic tradition. He uses specific literary forms and particular items of apocalyptic tradition that can also be traced in the Jewish apocalypses.[4] But for our purposes, it is more impor-

---

[2] J. J. Collins, 'Introduction: Towards the Morphology of a Genre', *Semeia* 14 (1979), 9.

[3] See especially C. Rowland, *The Open Heaven* (London: SPCK, 1982).

[4] For examples of Jewish apocalyptic traditions in Revelation, see R. Bauckham, 'Resurrection as Giving Back the Dead: A Traditional Image of Resurrection in the Pseudepigrapha and the Apocalypse of John', forthcoming in J. H. Charlesworth and C. A. Evans, eds., *The Pseudepigrapha and the New Testament: Comparative*

tant to indicate two very broad ways in whic
stands in the tradition of Jewish apocalyptic litei

In the first place, John's work is a prophetic
that it communicates a disclosure of a transcende
on this world. It is prophetic in the way it addresses a concrete
historical situation – that of Christians in the Roman province
of Asia towards the end of the first century AD – and brings to
its readers a prophetic word of God, enabling them to discern
the divine purpose in their situation and respond to their
situation in a way appropriate to this purpose. This contextual
communication of the divine purpose is typical of the biblical
prophetic tradition. But John's work is also *apocalyptic*, because
the way that it enables its readers to see their situation with
prophetic insight into God's purpose is by disclosing the
content of a vision in which John is taken, as it were, out of this
world in order to see it differently. Here John's work belongs to
the apocalyptic tradition of visionary disclosure, in which a
seer is taken in vision to God's throne-room in heaven to learn
the secrets of the divine purpose (cf., e.g., 1 Enoch 14–16; 46;
60:1–6; 71; 2 Enoch 20–1; Ap. Abr. 9–18).

John (and thereby his readers with him) is taken up into
heaven in order to see the world from the heavenly perspective.
He is given a glimpse behind the scenes of history so that he can
see what is really going on in the events of his time and place.
He is also transported in vision into the final future of the
world, so that he can see the present from the perspective of
what its final outcome must be, in God's ultimate purpose for
human history. The effect of John's visions, one might say, is to
expand his readers' world, both spatially (into heaven) and
temporally (into the eschatological future), or, to put it
another way, to open their world to divine transcendence. The
bounds which Roman power and ideology set to the readers'
world are broken open and that world is seen as open to the
greater purpose of its transcendent Creator and Lord. It is not

Studies (to appear in the *Journal for the Study of the Pseudepigrapha* Supplement Series;
Sheffield Academic Press, 1992); and chapter 2 ('The Use of Apocalyptic Tradi-
tions') in R. Bauckham, *The Climax of Prophecy: Studies in the Book of Revelation*
(Edinburgh: T. & T. Clark, 1992).

.nat the here-and-now are left behind in an escape into heaven or the eschatological future, but that the here-and-now look quite different when they are opened to transcendence.

The world seen from this transcendent perspective, in apocalyptic vision, is a kind of new symbolic world into which John's readers are taken as his artistry creates it for them.[5] But really it is not another world. It is John's readers' concrete, day-to-day world seen in heavenly and eschatological perspective. As such its function, as we shall notice in more detail later, is to counter the Roman imperial view of the world, which was the dominant ideological perception of their situation that John's readers naturally tended to share. Revelation counters that false view of reality by opening the world to divine transcendence. All that it shares with the apocalyptic literature by way of the motifs of visionary transportation to heaven, visions of God's throne-room in heaven, angelic mediators of revelation, symbolic visions of political powers, coming judgment and new creation – all this serves the purpose of revealing the world in which John's readers live in the perspective of the transcendent divine purpose.

A second important sense in which Revelation stands in the tradition of the Jewish apocalypses is that it shares the *question* which concerned so many of the latter: who is Lord over the world? Jewish apocalypses, insofar as they continued the concerns of the Old Testament prophetic tradition, were typically concerned with the apparent non-fulfilment of God's promises, through the prophets, for the judgment of evil, the salvation of the righteous, the achievement of God's righteous rule over his world. The righteous suffer, the wicked flourish: the world seems to be ruled by evil, not by God. Where is God's kingdom? The apocalyptists sought to maintain the faith of God's people in the one, all-powerful and righteous God, in the face of the harsh realities of evil in the world, especially the political evil of the oppression of God's faithful people by the great pagan empires. The answer to this problem was always, essentially, that, despite appearances, it is God who rules his

[5] See D. L. Barr, 'The Apocalypse as a Symbolic Transformation of the World: A Literary Analysis', *Int.* 38 (1984), 39–50.

creation and the time is coming soon when he will overthrow the evil empires and establish his kingdom.[6] John's apocalypse in important ways shares that central apocalyptic concern. He sees God's rule over the world apparently contradicted by the rule of the Roman Empire, which arrogates divine rule over the world to itself and to all appearances does so successfully. He faces the question: who then is really Lord of this world? He anticipates the eschatological crisis in which the issue will come to a head and be resolved in God's ultimate triumph over all evil and his establishment of his eternal kingdom. How John deals with these themes is significantly distinctive, as we shall see, but the distinctiveness emerges from his continuity with the concerns of the Jewish apocalyptic tradition.

DIFFERENCES FROM OTHER APOCALYPSES

At this point, having fully recognized that Revelation belongs to the literary genre of the apocalypse, we should notice two purely formal, literary ways in which it is distinctive when compared with other apocalypses. The first is rarely noticed. John's work is highly unusual in the sheer prolific extent of its visual imagery. It is true that symbolic visions are typical of the genre. But in other apocalypses other forms of revelation are often as important or more important. There are often long conversations between the seer and the heavenly revealer (God or his angel), in which information is conveyed in terms quite different from the visual symbols that dominate Revelation (cf., e.g., 4 Ezra 3–10; 2 Bar. 10–30). There are often long passages of narrative prophecy (e.g. Dan. 11:2–12:4), of which Revelation has very little (cf. 11:5–13; 20:7–10). The proportion of visual symbolism in Revelation is greater than in almost any comparable apocalypse. But there are further differences beside the proportion. Symbolic visions in the apocalypses commonly have to be interpreted by an angel who explains their meaning to the seer (e.g. 4 Ezra 10:38–54; 12:10–36; 13:21–56; 2 Bar. 56–74). Such interpretations are rare in

[6] See, e.g., R. Bauckham, 'The Rise of Apocalyptic', *Them.* 3/2 (1978), 10–23; Rowland, *Open Heaven*, 126–35.

Revelation (7:13–14; 17:6–18), whose visual symbols are so described as to convey their own meaning. The symbols can thus retain a surplus of meaning which any translation into literal terms runs the risk of reducing.

Furthermore, the kind of symbolic vision which is typical of the apocalypses is relatively short and self-contained, comprising just one section of an apocalypse (e.g. Dan. 7; 8; 4 Ezra 10; 11–12; 13). The imagery of such a vision will be peculiar to it, not recurring in other parts of the apocalypse. Revelation, by contrast, is really (from 1:10 to 22:6) a single vision. The imagery is common to the whole. From time to time the scene shifts and fresh images may be introduced, but, once introduced, they may recur throughout the book. Thus John's vision creates a single symbolic universe in which its readers may live for the time it takes them to read (or hear) the book. Both the profusion of the visual imagery and the unity and continuity of the visionary sequence make Revelation distinctive among the apocalypses.

This is not to be explained simply by supposing that John had a remarkably powerful visual imagination. The power, the profusion and the consistency of the symbols have a literary–theological purpose. They create a symbolic world which readers can enter so fully that it affects them and changes their perception of the world. Most 'readers' were originally, of course, hearers. Revelation was designed for oral enactment in Christian worship services (cf. 1:3).[7] Its effect would therefore be somewhat comparable to a dramatic performance, in which the audience enter the world of the drama for its duration and can have their perception of the world outside the drama powerfully shifted by their experience of the world of the drama. Many of the apocalypses could have something of this effect. But Revelation's peculiarly visual character and peculiar symbolic unity give it a particular potential for communicating in this way. It is an aspect of the book to which we shall return.

A second formal, literary difference between Revelation and

[7] See D. L. Barr, 'The Apocalypse of John as Oral Enactment', *Int.* 40 (1986) 243–56.

the Jewish apocalypses is that, unlike the latter, Revelation is not pseudepigraphal. The writers of Jewish apocalypses did not write in their own names, but under the name of some ancient seer of the biblical tradition, such as Enoch, Abraham or Ezra. The explanation for this phenomenon is not easy to discern.[8] It is unlikely that the authors of the apocalypses seriously intended to deceive, more probable that they wished to claim the authority of an ancient tradition, in which they felt themselves to stand, rather than an independent authority of their own. But pseudepigraphy had an important literary consequence. The authors of apocalypses had to set them fictionally in a situation in the distant past. Of course, they were writing for their own contemporaries and with their own situation in view, but they could not do so explicitly, except by representing the apocalyptic seer as foreseeing the distant future, the period at the end of the age in which the real author and his readers lived.

By contrast, John writes in his own name. He is certainly very conscious of writing within the tradition of the Old Testament prophets, but he is himself a prophet within that tradition. Since he stands at the culmination of the whole tradition, on the brink of the final eschatological fulfilment to which all prophecy had ultimately pointed, his authority is if anything greater than that of his predecessors. Of course, the authority really resides not in himself but in the revelation of Jesus Christ to which he bears prophetic witness (1:1–2). But his prophetic consciousness is such that, like Isaiah or Ezekiel, he feels no need of pseudonymity but writes in his own name (1:1, 4, 9; 22:8) and relates his own commissioning to prophesy (1:10–11, 19; 10:8–11).

It is instructive to compare 22:10 with the verses on which it is modelled, at the end of the book of Daniel, the canonical apocalypse to which John's prophecy is much indebted.[9] The angel tells Daniel: 'keep the words secret and the book sealed

---

[8] See, e.g., D. S. Russell, *The Method and Message of Jewish Apocalyptic* (London: SCM Press, 1964), 127–39; Rowland, *Open Heaven*, 240–5; D. G. Meade, *Pseudonymity and Canon* (WUNT 39; Tübingen: Mohr (Siebeck), 1986), chapter 4.

[9] G. K. Beale, *The Use of Daniel in Jewish Apocalyptic Literature and in the Revelation of St John* (Lanham, New York and London: University of America Press, 1984).

until the time of the end ... Go your way, Daniel, for the words
are to remain secret and sealed until the time of the end' (Dan.
12:4, 9). Daniel's visions relate to a future distant from the time
in which Daniel lived. His prophecy is to remain secret, hidden
in a sealed book, until the time of the end when the people who
live at that time will be able to understand it. John's angel
gives strikingly different instructions: 'Do not seal up the words
of the prophecy of this book, for the time is near' (22:10; cf.
1:3). John's prophecy is of immediate relevance to his contemporaries. It relates not to a distant future but to the situation John himself shares with his contemporaries in the seven
churches of Asia. Hence he evokes this situation at the opening
of his prophecy: 'I John, your brother who share with you in
Jesus the persecution and the kingdom and the patient endurance ...' (1:9). Hence he addresses, not just the seven messages
of chapters 2–3, but the whole book to his contemporaries in
the seven churches of Asia (1:4, 11). It is their situation which
is the eschatological situation on which the end of history
immediately impinges.

This explicit contemporaneity of John with his readers
means that he can address their actual situation not only more
explicitly but also with more concreteness and particularity
than was possible for apocalyptists writing under an ancient
pseudonym. This brings us back to the third literary genre to
which Revelation belongs: the letter.

REVELATION AS A CIRCULAR LETTER

The whole book of Revelation is a circular letter addressed to
seven specific churches: Ephesus, Smyrna, Pergamum, Thyatira, Sardis, Philadelphia, Laodicea (1:11; cf. 1:4; 22:16). They
are probably named in the order in which they would be
visited by a messenger starting from Patmos and travelling on a
circular route around the province of Asia. But many misread-
ings of Revelation, especially those which assume that much of
the book was not addressed to its first-century readers and
could only be understood by later generations, have resulted
from neglecting the fact that it is a letter.

The special character of a letter as a literary genre is that it enables the writer to specify those to whom he or she is writing and to address their situation as specifically as he or she may wish. Writings in most other literary genres are in principle addressed to a much less clearly defined audience: anyone who might plausibly be expected to read the work. Letters may, of course, prove of interest and value to readers beyond the circle of the specified addressees. This is how some apostolic letters, such as Paul's, came to circulate to churches other than those to which they were originally sent and eventually became part of the New Testament canon. A letter-writer such as Paul might even *expect* his letter to be passed on to readers other than those he addresses (cf. Col. 4:16). But it remains the case that such readers are not actually addressed. The more specifically the content of the letter relates to the concerns and situation of its addressees, the more other readers have to read it as a letter not to themselves, but to other people. This need not diminish its value to readers other than the addressees. 1 Corinthians, for example, deals very specifically with problems in the church at Corinth at the time of writing, but it has proved valuable to very many other readers. Such readers read it appropriately when they take account of the fact that it was written to the Corinthian church. It can speak to them, but only when something of the context of its original addressees becomes part of the way it speaks to them.

A circular letter could not usually be as specific as a letter to a single group of addressees could be. One need only compare Paul's letters to specific churches with Ephesians (probably originally a circular letter to a number of churches) or 1 Peter, to realize the difference. In Revelation, however, John has employed an apparently original method of writing a circular letter which speaks as specifically as could be desired to each particular church. While most of his work is intended for all the churches indiscriminately, he introduces it with a series of seven specific messages from Christ to the seven churches (chapters 2–3). Each message is specifically relevant to the situation of the church addressed, which John knew well. These seven messages show us that the seven churches were very different, facing different problems and reacting very differently to common problems. Christ speaks individually to each church. But the messages are not self-contained. Each is an introduction to the rest of the book.

That the seven messages are introductory to the rest of the book can be seen especially from the promises to the conquerors which complete each message: Christ makes a promise of eschatological salvation (specified in terms which usually have some special appropriateness to the church addressed) to 'the one who conquers' (2: 7, 11, 17, 26–8; 3:5, 12, 21). In each of the very different church situations, the call is to be victorious. But the meaning of victory is unexplained. What it is to conquer becomes clear only from the rest of the book, in which the conquerors appear and it is revealed what they conquer and in what their victory consists. Then the formula of the promises to the conquerors, used in each of the seven messages, reappears just once, in the vision of the new Jerusalem (21:7). Thus the call to conquer, addressed to the Christians in each of the seven churches in chapters 2–3, is a call to engage in the eschatological battle described in the central chapters of the book, in order to reach the eschatological destiny described at the end of the book. In a sense the whole book is about the way the Christians of the seven churches may, by being victorious within the specific situations of their own churches, enter the new Jerusalem. While the book as a whole explains what the war is about and how it must be won, the message to each church alerts that church to what is specific about its section of the battlefield.

So the seven messages provide seven different introductions to the rest of the book. John has designed a book which, very unusually, is intended to be read from seven explicitly different perspectives, though of course these are perspectives within a broader common situation which all seven churches share. Although Revelation after chapters 2–3 is not specific to the situation of any one church, it is specific to their common situation as Christian churches in the Roman Empire towards the end of the first century AD. The device of the seven messages enables John to engage appropriately with seven different contexts in which his book would be read and also to integrate those contexts into the broader perspective of the rest of the book, in which John is concerned with the worldwide tyranny of Rome and, even more broadly, with the cosmic conflict of God and evil and the eschatological purpose of God for his whole creation. In this way he shows the Christians of each of the seven churches how the issues in their local context belong to, and must be understood in the light of, God's cosmic battle against evil and his eschatological purpose of establishing his kingdom.

The fact that John explicitly and carefully contextualizes his prophetic message in seven specific contexts makes it possible for us to resist a common generalization about Revelation: that it is a book written for the consolation and encouragement of Christians suffering persecution, in order to assure them that their oppressors will be judged and they will be vindicated in the end. The common, uncritical acceptance of this generalization probably has to do with the fact that it is a generalization often made about apocalyptic literature as a whole.[10] We need not discuss here how far apocalyptic literature in general functions as consolation for the oppressed, because in the case of Revelation it is quite clear from the seven messages that encouragement in the face of oppression was only one of the needs of the seven churches. The messages show that John addresses a variety of situations which he perceives as very different. By no means all of his readers were poor and persecuted by an oppressive system: many were affluent and compromising with the oppressive system. The latter are offered not consolation and encouragement, but severe warnings and calls to repent. For these Christians, the judgments which are so vividly described in the rest of the book should appear not as judgments on their enemies so much as judgments they themselves were in danger of incurring, since worshipping the beast was not something only their pagan neighbours did. Worshipping the beast was something many of John's Christian readers were tempted to do or were actually doing or even (if they

[10] E.g. Russell, *Method and Message*, 17.

listened, for example, to the prophet 'Jezebel' at Thyatira) justified. Whether the visions bring consolation and encouragement or warning and painful challenge depends on which of the groups of Christians depicted in the seven messages a reader belongs to. Moreover, as we shall see in chapter 4 of this book, the call to 'conquer' which is addressed to all the churches in the seven messages, transcends both consolation and warning. It calls Christians to a task of witnessing to God and his righteousness for which the consolations and warnings of the seven messages are designed to prepare them.

Once we have fully recognized the specificity of the seven messages to the churches, it is possible to ask whether John also envisaged other readers. Why does he write to *seven* churches? These were by no means the only Christian churches in the province of Asia, and John must surely have expected his work to be passed on from these seven to other churches in the area and even farther afield. The definitiveness with which he seems to envisage his prophecy as the final culmination of the whole biblical prophetic tradition suggests a relevance for all Christian churches. This is what the number seven must indicate. We shall observe quite often in this book the symbolic significance which attaches to numbers in Revelation. Seven is the number of completeness.[11] By addressing seven churches John indicates that his message is addressed to specific churches as *representative* of *all* the churches. This conclusion is confirmed by the refrain – a summons to attend to a prophetic oracle – which occurs in each of the seven messages: 'Let anyone who has an ear listen to what the Spirit is saying to the churches' (2:7, 11, 17, 29; 3:6, 13, 22). This seems to invite all readers to listen to the message addressed to each of the seven churches. It does not diminish the specificity of what is said to each church, as peculiarly relevant to that particular church. It means that precisely by addressing very specifically a variety of actual church situations, Revelation addresses a *representative* variety of contexts. The range of different situations in these seven churches is sufficient for any Christian church in the late

---

[11] Note the way that the Muratorian Canon claims that both John (in Revelation) and Paul actually wrote to *all* churches by writing to seven.

first century to find analogies to its own situation in one or more of the messages and therefore to find the whole book relevant to itself. Churches in later periods have been able to do the same, allowing for a necessary degree of adjustment to changing historical contexts.

UNDERSTANDING THE IMAGERY

We have already noticed the unusual profusion of visual imagery in Revelation and its capacity to create a symbolic world which its readers can enter and thereby have their perception of the world in which they lived transformed. To appreciate the importance of this we should remember that Revelation's readers in the great cities of the province of Asia were constantly confronted with powerful images of the Roman vision of the world. Civic and religious architecture, iconography, statues, rituals and festivals, even the visual wonder of cleverly engineered 'miracles' (cf. Rev. 13:13–14) in the temples[12] – all provided powerful visual impressions of Roman imperial power and of the splendour of pagan religion.[13] In this context, Revelation provides a set of Christian prophetic counter-images which impress on its readers a different vision of the world: how it looks from the heaven to which John is caught up in chapter 4. The visual power of the book effects a kind of purging of the Christian imagination, refurbishing it with alternative visions of how the world is and will be. For example, in chapter 17 John's readers share his vision of a woman. At first glance, she might seem to be the goddess Roma, in all her glory, a stunning personification of the civilization of Rome, as she was worshipped in many a temple in the cities of Asia.[14] But as John sees her, she is a Roman prostitute,

[12] S. J. Scherrer, 'Signs and Wonders in the Imperial Cult: A New Look at a Roman Religious Institution in the Light of Rev 13:13–15', *JBL* 103 (1984), 599–610.

[13] See P. J. J. Botha, 'God, Emperor Worship and Society: Contemporary Experiences and the Book of Revelation', *Neot.* 22 (1988), 87–102.

[14] Cf. D. Magie, *Roman Rule in Asia Minor to the End of the Third Century after Christ* (Princeton University Press, 1950), 1613–14; S. R. F. Price, *Rituals and Power: The Roman Imperial Cult in Asia Minor* (Cambridge University Press, 1984), 40–3, 252, 254; R. Mellor, *ΘΕΑ ΡѠΜΗ: The Worship of the Goddess Roma in the Greek World* (Hypomnemata 42; Göttingen: Vandenhoeck & Ruprecht, 1975), 79–82.

a seductive whore and a scheming witch, and her wealth and splendour represent the profits of her disreputable trade. For good measure there are biblical overtones of the harlot queen Jezebel to reinforce the impression. In this way, John's readers are able to perceive something of Rome's true character – her moral corruption behind the enticing propagandist illusions of Rome which they constantly encountered in their cities.

It should be clear that the images of Revelation are symbols with evocative power inviting imaginative participation in the book's symbolic world. But they do not work merely by painting verbal pictures. Their precise literary composition is always essential to their meaning. In the first place, the astonishingly meticulous composition of the book creates a complex network of literary cross-references, parallels, contrasts, which inform the meaning of the parts and the whole. Naturally, not all of these will be noticed on first or seventh or seventieth reading. They are one of the ways in which the book is designed to yield its rich store of meaning progressively through intensive study. Secondly, as we have already noticed, Revelation is saturated with verbal allusions to the Old Testament. These are not incidental but essential to the way meaning is conveyed. Without noticing some of the key allusions, little if anything of the meaning of the images will be understood. But like the literary patterning, John's very precise and subtle use of Old Testament allusions creates a reservoir of meaning which can be progressively tapped. The Old Testament allusions frequently presuppose their Old Testament context and a range of connexions between Old Testament texts which are not made explicit but lie beneath the surface of the text of Revelation. If we wonder what the average Christian in the churches of Asia could make of this, we should remember that the strongly Jewish character of most of these churches made the Old Testament much more familiar than it is even to well-educated modern Christians. But we should also remember the circle of Christian prophets in the churches (cf. 22:9, 16) who would probably have studied, interpreted and expounded John's prophecy with the same kind of learned attention they gave to the Old Testament prophecies.

As well as their pervasive allusion to the Old Testament, the images of Revelation also echo mythological images from its contemporary world. The serpent or the dragon, Revelation's symbol for the primeval source of evil in the world, the devil (12:3–9), is a good example of a symbol with strong biblical roots (Gen. 3:14–15; Isa. 27:1) which Revelation evokes, but also with wide cultural resonances in the minds of contemporary readers, owing to its prominence in pagan mythology and religion.[15] Another type of contemporary allusion is the idea of invasion from the East (9:13–19; 16:12). Here John takes up a very real political fear in the Roman Empire in the first century AD, since the threat of invasion from the Parthian Empire was widely felt. It had the same kind of overtones of conquest by a cruel and alien civilization which the threat of Russian invasion had for many western Europeans in the period of the Cold War, though for some of Rome's eastern subjects it offered the prospect of liberation from Roman oppression. When Revelation pictures the kings of the East invading the Empire in alliance with 'the beast who was and is not and is about to ascend from the bottomless pit' (17:8), it is echoing the contemporary myth which pictured the emperor Nero – remembered by some as a villainous tyrant, transfigured by others into a saviour-figure – returning one day at the head of the Parthian hordes to conquer the Roman Empire.[16] In ways such as these, John's images echo and play on the facts, the fears, the hopes, the imaginings and the myths of his contemporaries, in order to transmute them into elements of his own Christian prophetic meaning.

Thus it would be a serious mistake to understand the images of Revelation as timeless symbols. Their character conforms to the contextuality of Revelation as a letter to the seven churches of Asia. Their resonances in the specific social, political, cultural and religious world of their first readers need to be understood if their meaning is to be appropriated today. They

[15] R. Bauckham, 'The *Figurae* of John of Patmos', in Ann Williams, ed., *Prophecy and Millenarianism: Essays in Honour of Marjorie Reeves* (London: Longman, 1980), 116–21; in revised form: chapter 6 ('The Lion, the Lamb and the Dragon') in Bauckham, *The Climax of Prophecy*.

[16] See chapter 11 ('Nero and the Beast') in Bauckham, *The Climax of Prophecy*.

do not create a purely self-contained aesthetic world with no reference outside itself, but intend to relate to the world in which the readers live in order to reform and to redirect the readers' response to that world. However, if the images are not timeless symbols, but relate to the 'real' world, we need also to avoid the opposite mistake of taking them too literally as descriptive of the 'real' world and of predicted events in the 'real' world. They are not just a system of codes waiting to be translated into matter-of-fact references to people and events. Once we begin to appreciate their sources and their rich symbolic associations, we realize that they cannot be read either as literal descriptions or as encoded literal descriptions, but must be read for their theological meaning and their power to evoke response.

Consider, for example, the descriptions of the plagues of the seven trumpets (8:6–9:21) and the seven bowls (16:1–21). These form a highly schematized literary pattern which itself conveys meaning. Their content suggests, among many other things, the plagues of Egypt which accompanied the exodus, the fall of Jericho to the army of Joshua, the army of locusts depicted in the prophecy of Joel, the Sinai theophany, the contemporary fear of invasion by Parthian cavalry, the earthquakes to which the cities of Asia Minor were rather frequently subject, and very possibly the eruption of Vesuvius which had recently terrified the Mediterranean world.[17] John has taken some of his contemporaries' worst experiences and worst fears of wars and natural disasters, blown them up to apocalyptic proportions, and cast them in biblically allusive terms. The point is not to predict a sequence of events. The point is to evoke and to explore the meaning of the divine judgment which is impending on the sinful world.

The last of the seven bowls results in the fall of Babylon in an earthquake of unprecedented proportions (16:17–21). If we took this as literal prediction, we should soon find it contra-

---

[17] For these allusions, see, as well as the commentaries, J. M. Court, *Myth and History in the Book of Revelation* (London: SPCK, 1979), chapter 3; R. Bauckham, 'The Eschatological Earthquake in the Apocalypse of John', *Novum Testamentum* 19 (1977), 224–33, which becomes chapter 7 ('The Eschatological Earthquake') in Bauckham, *The Climax of Prophecy*.

dicted by later images of the downfall of Babylon. In 17:16, Babylon, now portrayed as a harlot, is stripped, devoured and burned by the beast and the ten kings. The traditional punishment of a harlot is here superimposed on the image of a city sacked and razed to the ground by an army. Chapter 18 extends the image of a city besieged and burned to the ground (cf. especially 18:8: 'pestilence ... famine ... burned with fire'), but we are also told both that the site of the city becomes the haunt of the desert creatures (18:2) and that the smoke from her burning continues to ascend for ever (19:3). On the literal level, these images are quite inconsistent with each other, but on the level of theological meaning, conveyed by the allusions to the Old Testament and to contemporary myth, they offer complementary perspectives on the meaning of Babylon's fall. The earthquake of 16:17–21 is that which accompanies the theophany of the holy God coming to final judgment. The sacking of Babylon by the beast and his allies alludes to the contemporary myth of the return of Nero to destroy Rome. It is an image of the self-destructive nature of evil, which on the level of theological meaning is not inconsistent with the idea of the destruction of evil by divine judgment but presents it under another aspect. The fire of 17:16 becomes in chapter 18 the fire of divine judgment, of which the paradigmatic Old Testament instance was the destruction of Sodom and Gomorrah. Like an apocalyptic Sodom sunk in the eternal lake of fire and sulphur, Babylon's smoke ascends for ever (cf. Gen. 19:28; Rev. 14:10–11; 19:20). The desolation of Babylon as a haunt of desert creatures evokes Old Testament prophetic pictures of the fate of both Edom and Babylon, the two great enemies of the people of God in much of Old Testament prophecy. All this – with much more in these chapters – makes up a wonderfully varied but coherent evocation of the biblical and theological meaning of the divine judgment John's prophecy pronounces on Rome; but if we try to read it as prediction of how that judgment will occur we turn it into a confused muddle and miss its real point.

Perhaps enough has been said to indicate that the imagery of Revelation requires close and appropriate study if modern readers are to grasp much of its theological meaning. Misunderstandings of the nature of the imagery and the way it conveys meaning account for many misinterpretations of Revelation, even by careful and learned modern scholars. In this book, we need especially to stress the way John has developed his literary use of imagery into a distinctive mode of theological thought and communication. Because Revelation does not contain theological discourse or argument of the kind with which readers of the New Testament are familiar in, for example, the Pauline letters, it should not be thought to be any less a product of profound theological reflection. Its images are by no means a vaguer or more impressionistic means of expression than the relatively more abstract conceptual argument of a Pauline letter. They are capable both of considerable precision of meaning and of compressing a wealth of meaning into a brief space by evoking a range of associations. The method and conceptuality of the theology of Revelation are relatively different from the rest of the New Testament, but once they are appreciated in their own right, Revelation can be seen to be not only one of the finest literary works in the New Testament, but also one of the greatest theological achievements of early Christianity. Moreover, the literary and theological greatness are not separable.

CHAPTER 2

The One who is and who was and who is to come

The theology of Revelation is highly theocentric. This, along with its distinctive doctrine of God, is its greatest contribution to New Testament theology. Our study of it must begin with God and will both constantly and finally return to God.

THE DIVINE TRINITY

Almost from the outset of his work John depicts the divine in threefold terms:

> Grace to you and peace
> from him who is and who was and who is to come,
> and from the seven Spirits who are before his throne,
> and from Jesus Christ, the faithful witness, the firstborn from
>   the dead, and the ruler of the kings of the earth.
>
> (1:4b–5a)

These words are a formal part of the form of letter-opening which is used in verses 4–5. Following the statement of writer and addressees, ancient letters gave a 'salutation', which in Jewish letters took the form of desiring blessings from God for the addressees. Early Christian practice often gave a specific-ally Christian character to this form by specifying the divine source of blessings as God and Jesus Christ. The standard form in the Pauline letters is: 'Grace to you and peace from God our Father and the Lord Jesus Christ' (e.g. Rom. 1:7; 1 Cor. 1:3; 2 Cor. 1:2; Gal. 1:3; Eph. 1:2). This form is of considerable theological significance. It places Jesus Christ with God on the divine side of the distinction between the divine Giver of

blessings and the creaturely recipients of blessings. It shows
how naturally early Christians implicitly included Jesus in the
divine, because he was the source of the salvation that comes
from God to humans, even if they had no way of conceptualiz-
ing in ontological terms this relation of Jesus to God.

Among early Christian letter-openings, John's is unique in
giving the standard form of salutation a 'trinitarian' character.
There are 'trinitarian' formulae elsewhere in early Christian
literature, even in letter-openings (e.g. 1 Pet. 1:2), but the
'trinitarian' form of John's salutation is unique. It is highly
probable that it is his own original adaptation of the standard
form: 'Grace to you and peace from God our Father and the
Lord Jesus Christ.' This is supported by the fact that he also
adapts the form by substituting for 'God our Father' and 'the
Lord Jesus Christ' descriptions of God and Jesus which are
highly distinctive of his own usage elsewhere in Revelation. All
this suggests, as much else in the book will confirm, that John
has reflected creatively on the Christian understanding of the
divine. Far from taking over unreflectively conventional early
Christian ways of speaking of God, Christ and the Spirit, he
has forged his own distinctive forms of God-language, not, of
course, *de novo*, but by creative use of the resources of Jewish
and Jewish Christian tradition. His book is the product of a
highly reflective consciousness of God. Any account of its
theology must give priority, as it does, to its distinctive ways of
speaking of the divine.

John's original variation of the salutation in 1:4b–5a
strongly suggests that his understanding of the divine is
deliberately 'trinitarian'. I put the word in inverted commas
only to warn us that, of course, we must not attribute to John
the particular conceptuality of the patristic doctrine of the
Trinity which became the norm for the later Christian tradition. As we shall see in the next two chapters, the theological
concern that gives John's understanding of the divine a trinitarian character is fundamentally the same as that which led to
the patristic development of trinitarian doctrine: a concern to
include Jesus, as well as the Spirit, in Jewish monotheistic faith
in God. But we must understand his response to this concern in

its own terms. Of course, it is hardly possible to describe and
analyse John's understanding of God without using language
he himself does not use. I have spoken of his 'trinitarian'
understanding of 'the divine', rather than 'of God', because he
himself, like most early Christian writers, restricts the word
'God' to God the Father of Jesus Christ, the One he here calls
'the One who is and who was and who is to come'. But 'the
divine' is hardly more satisfactory. John has no vocabulary
equivalent to later trinitarian talk of the divine nature which
three divine persons share. But it is impossible for us to do
justice to what he does say without speaking somehow of a
divine reality in which Jesus Christ and the Holy Spirit (here
symbolized by 'the seven Spirits')[1] are included.

The prominence John gives to a 'trinitarian' understanding
of the divine in 1:4b–5a may justify our use of a trinitarian
structure for the major part of our account of the theology of
Revelation (in our chapters 2–5). No such structure could be
wholly satisfactory, but this one at least corresponds to a major
feature of the theology of Revelation. However, for ease of
exposition we shall follow the order: God, Christ, Spirit (rather
than that of 1:4b–5).

THE ALPHA AND THE OMEGA

The prologue to Revelation ends with a divine self-declaration:

'I am the Alpha and the Omega', says the Lord God, who is and who
was and who is to come, the Almighty.

(1:8)

This strategically placed verse incorporates three of the four
most important designations for God in Revelation: 'the Alpha
and the Omega', 'the Lord God Almighty' and 'the One who is
and who was and who is to come'. It stands out not only by its
position immediately preceding the beginning of John's
account of his vision (1:9–22:6), but also because it is one of
only two occasions in Revelation on which God himself speaks.
The second occasion (21:5–8) includes a similar divine self-

[1] See chapter 5 below.

declaration: 'I am the Alpha and the Omega, the beginning
and the end' (21:6).

But these two divine self-declarations correspond to two
self-declarations by Jesus Christ. The pattern is as follows:

God: I am the Alpha and the Omega.

(1:8)

Christ: I am the first and the last.

(1:17)

God: I am the Alpha and the Omega, the beginning and the end.
(21:6)

Christ: I am the Alpha and the Omega, the first and the last, the
        beginning and the end.

(22:13)

We leave to the next chapter a discussion of the full significance
of this pattern and the remarkable fact that the one designation
of God which appears in Revelation as a self-designation by
God also appears as a self-designation by Christ. Here we shall
confine ourselves to the designation as applied to God. But
comparison of the four passages shows that the three phrases –
the Alpha and the Omega, the first and the last, the beginning
and the end – are very probably to be considered equivalent.
Since Alpha and Omega are the first and last letters of the
Greek alphabet, it is not difficult to see that 'the Alpha and the
Omega' is equivalent in meaning to 'the first and the last' and
'the beginning and the end'. The pattern also shows that, if the
three phrases are treated as equivalent, then Revelation contains seven occurrences of them in self-declarations by God and
Christ (not counting the additional occurrence of 'the first and
the last' in 2:8, where it echoes the use in 1:17). The number is
not likely to be accidental, since, as we shall see, two of the
other three most important designations for God in Revelation
also occur seven times. Numerical patterns have theological
significance in Revelation. Seven is the number of completeness. Just as the seven beatitudes scattered through the
book (1:3; 14:13; 16:15; 19:9; 20:6; 22:7; 14) indicate the
fullness of blessing to be bestowed on the reader or hearer who

faithfully obeys the message of Revelation, so the sevenfold occurrence of a significant divine title indicates the fullness of the divine being to which that title points. Theological meaning is thus written into the detail of John's meticulous literary composition.

In the form, 'the first and the last', the designation derives from Isaiah, where it occurs, as in Revelation, as a divine self-designation: 'I am the first and the last; besides me there is no god' (44:6); 'I am he; I am the first, and I am the last' (48:12; cf. also 41:4). In those chapters of Isaiah (now known as Deutero-Isaiah) the designation encapsulates the understanding of the God of Israel as the sole Creator of all things and sovereign Lord of history, which Deutero-Isaiah so magnificently expounds and asserts polemically against the idols of Babylon. Unlike human-made gods, this God is the utterly incomparable One, to whom all nations are subject, whose purpose none can frustrate (cf. Isa. 40:12–26). It is precisely this exclusive monotheistic faith that determines the prophetic outlook of Revelation. Hence the unique importance of the designation: 'the Alpha and the Omega'. God precedes all things, as their Creator, and he will bring all things to eschatological fulfilment. He is the origin and goal of all history. He has the first word, in creation, and the last word, in new creation. Therefore, within John's literary structure, he speaks twice, declaring himself Alpha and Omega first, before the outset of John's vision (1:8), and last, in declaring the eschatological accomplishment of his purpose for his whole creation: 'it is done!' (21:6).

The form, 'the beginning and the end', had been used in the Greek philosophical tradition to indicate the eternity of the supreme God, and was taken over by Jewish writers, such as Josephus, who calls God 'the beginning and the end of all things' (*Ant.* 8.280; cf. Philo, *Plant.* 93). That John gives priority to the phrase 'the Alpha and the Omega' over both of its two equivalents may be because he connects the former with the divine name. The biblical name of God YHWH was sometimes vocalized Yāhôh and so transliterated into Greek (which has no consonant 'h') as IAⲰ (Iota, Alpha, Omega).[2] In the context of Jewish theological speculation about the divine name, the occurrence of the first and last letters of the Greek alphabet in this Greek form of the name could have suggested that the name itself contains the implication that God is the first and the last. A connexion with the divine name is the more likely in that the next divine designation we shall consider, which also occurs in 1:8, is certainly intended as an interpretation of the meaning of the name.

THE ONE WHO IS AND WHO WAS AND WHO IS TO COME

This designation of God occurs, with variation, five times:

1:4:	the One who is and who was and who is to come.
1:8:	the One who is and who was and who is to come.
4:8:	the One who was and who is and who is to come.
11:17:	the One who is and who was.
16:5:	the One who is and who was.

Again there is a numerical pattern here, which is likely to be deliberate: the form with three tenses is used three times, the form with two tenses twice.

This designation is an interpretation of the divine name YHWH. In the Old Testament itself, the only interpretation of the name is found in Exodus 3:14, which associates it with the verb 'to be', and interprets it first by the enigmatic phrase 'I am who I am' (or: 'I will be who I will be': *'ehyeh '^{a}šer 'ehyeh*), and then simply as 'I am' (*'ehyeh*). Later Jewish interpretation understood these interpretations as statements of the divine eternity. Thus Philo(*Mos.* 1.75) understands the divine name to be 'the one who is' (*ho ōn*), which expresses the divine eternity in hellenistic philosophical fashion as timeless being. Alternatively, the meaning could be unpacked in terms of past, present and future existence. This is how the Palestinian Targum (Pseudo-Jonathan) paraphrased the divine name: 'I am who I was and will be' (Exod. 3:14) or 'I am who is and

---

[2] E.g. the Hadrumetum magical text, quoted in E. Schürer, *The History of the Jewish People in the Age of Jesus Christ*, revised and ed. G. Vermes, F. Millar, M. Goodman, vol. III: 1 (Edinburgh: T. & T. Clark, 1986), 358.

who was, and I am who I will be' (Deut. 32:29; cf. also Sibylline Oracle 3:16). Formulae asserting existence in three tenses were also used of Greek gods or the supreme God of philosophy,[3] and this usage may well have influenced the Jewish interpretation of the divine name. But it must be on the latter that Revelation is directly dependent.

In the form John uses in 1:4, 8 (*ho ōn kai ho ēn kai ho erchomenos*) he agrees with the Targum in giving priority to God's present existence, but he significantly departs from all other instances, Jewish or Greek, of this threefold formula in that the third term is not the future of the verb 'to be' but the present participle of the verb 'to come' ('the one who is coming'). It is true that, as also in English, this can mean virtually 'future'. Thus, for example, 'the age to come' or 'the coming age' (*ho aiōn ho erchomenos*) means 'the future age'. But John has taken advantage of this usage to depict the future of God not as his mere future existence, but as his coming to the world in salvation and judgment. He no doubt has in mind those many Old Testament prophetic passages which announce that God will 'come' to save and judge (e.g. Ps. 96:13; 98:9; Isa. 40:10; 66:15; Zech. 14:5) and which early Christians understood to refer to his eschatological coming to fulfil his final purpose for the world, a coming they identified with the parousia of Jesus Christ.

This interpretation is confirmed by the use, in 11:17; 16:5, of the abbreviated form of the designation: 'the One who is and who was'. At these points in the vision the eschatological coming of God is taking place. It is no longer future, and the hymns which use the designation praise God for the occurrence of this eschatological fulfilment of his purpose. Especially clear is 11:17: 'We give you thanks, Lord God Almighty, who are and who were, for you have taken your great power and begun to reign.' The achievement of God's eschatological rule over the world is his coming. Necessarily the future element in the designation of God is replaced by the thanksgiving that his role has begun.

---

[3] *TDNT* 2.399; D. E. Aune, *Prophecy in Early Christianity and the Ancient Mediterranean World* (Grand Rapids: Eerdmans, 1983), 280–1.

Thus John interprets the divine name as indicating not God's eternity in himself apart from the world, but his eternity in relation to the world. This is the biblical God who chooses, as his own future, his coming to his creation, and whose creation will find its own future in him (cf. 21:3). Moreover, this interpretation of the divine name is in significant continuity with the meaning of Exodus 3:14, which most probably is referring not to God's self-existence purely in himself so much as to his commitment to be who he will be in his history with his people. John has characteristically developed that early Israelite faith in God's historical being for his people into the later, eschatological faith in God's final coming to bring all things to fulfilment in his eternal future.

THE LORD GOD THE ALMIGHTY

This designation occurs seven times in Revelation (1:8; 4:8; 11:17; 15:3; 16:7; 19:6; 21:22), four of these in close association (1:8; 4:8; 11:17) or close proximity (16:5–7) to the designation we have just discussed. A shorter form, 'God the Almighty', is used twice (16:14; 19:15), keeping the number of occurrences of the full expression to no more than the significant number seven.

This designation is also connected with the divine name, since it is a standard translation of the expanded form of the divine name: *YHWH 'elōhē (haṣ)ṣebā'ōt* (the LORD, the God of hosts') (e.g. 2 Sam. 5:10; Jer. 5:14; Hos. 12:5; Amos 3:13; 4:13). John also uses it (as comparison of Rev. 4:8 with Isa. 6:3 will show) as equivalent to the shorter form *YHWH ṣebā'ōt* ('the LORD of hosts'), which is very common in the Old Testament prophets because it indicates Yahweh's unrivalled power over all things and therefore his supremacy over the course of historical events. Its use in Revelation testifies to John's desire to continue the prophetic faith in God. The Greek *pantokratōr* ('almighty') indicates not so much God's abstract omnipotence as his actual control over all things.

THE ONE WHO SITS ON THE THRONE

This is the last of the four most important designations of God in Revelation. In this precise form it occurs seven times (4:9; 5:1; 7, 13; 6:16; 7:15; 21:5), though variations of it are also used (4:2, 3; 7:10; 19:4; cf. 20:11). In addition, the throne itself, on which God sits in heaven, is mentioned very frequently. It is one of the central symbols of the whole book. It indicates how decisive for the theological perspective of Revelation is faith in God's sovereignty over all things.

The significance of the image of the throne emerges especially in the vision of the divine throne-room in chapter 4. After the vision of the risen Christ with his people on earth (1:9–3:22), John is taken up into heaven (4:1). This gives the whole prophecy two starting-points: the situation of the seven churches, as perceived and addressed in Christ's messages to them, and the vision of God's sovereignty in heaven. It is the latter which makes it possible for John to enlarge his readers' perspective on their own situation by setting it within the broader context of God's universal purpose of overcoming all opposition to his rule and establishing his kingdom in the world. In chapter 4 God's sovereignty is seen as it is already fully acknowledged in heaven. This establishes it as the true reality which must in the end also prevail on earth. On earth the powers of evil challenge God's role and even masquerade as the ultimate power over all things, claiming divinity. But heaven is the sphere of ultimate reality: what is true in heaven must become true on earth. Thus John is taken up into heaven to see that God's throne is the ultimate reality behind all earthly appearances. Having seen God's sovereignty in heaven, he can then see how it must come to be acknowledged on earth.

Visions of the divine throne go far back into the Old Testament prophetic tradition (cf. 1 Kings 22:19–23) and were a significant feature of many of the Jewish apocalypses.[4] John writes within this tradition and in particular his vision, like

[4] Cf. Dan. 7:9–10; 1 Enoch 14; 60:1–6; 71; 2 Enoch 20–1; Ap. Abr. 15–18.

most of those in the apocalypses, draws on the two great
prophetic visions of the divine throne in Isaiah 6 and Ezekiel 1.
Also like the Jewish apocalyptists, John locates the divine
throne in heaven, where heavenly beings engaged in continuous worship surround it. There is nothing in chapter 4
which could not have been written by a non-Christian Jewish
visionary. Only in the continuation of the vision in chapter 5,
which introduces the Lamb, Jesus Christ, as the one who is to
bring God's rule into effect on earth, and which we shall
examine in our next chapter, does the specifically Jewish *Christian* character of Revelation's theology become apparent. But,
of course, the absence of distinctively Christian features from
chapter 4 by no means diminishes its foundational importance
for the theology of Revelation. In Revelation, as elsewhere in
the New Testament, the Christian faith in God presupposes
Jewish monotheism. It takes up the principal features of the
understanding of God in the Old Testament and later Jewish
tradition, without which it would be unintelligible, into a
distinctive theological development determined by Christology. The christological development will concern us in our
next chapter. Here we are concerned with the indispensable
expressions of Jewish monotheism in Revelation.

Like most apocalyptic visions of the divine throne, John's
does not dwell on the visible form of the One who sits on the
throne. All that is said of God's appearance is that it was like
precious stones (4:3): this was one of the traditional ways of
evoking the splendour of a heavenly figure. The unknowable
transcendence of God is protected by focussing instead on the
throne itself and what goes on around it. It is in these features
of the vision that what can be known of God is expressed.
Especially prominent in the vision is the continuous worship by
the four living creatures and the twenty-four elders. It is a
scene of worship into which the reader who shares John's faith
in God is almost inevitably drawn. We are thereby reminded
that true knowledge of who God is is inseparable from worship
of God. The song of the four living creatures and the hymn of
the twenty-four elders express the two most primary forms of
awareness of God: the awed perception of his numinous holi-

ness (4:8; cf. Isa. 6:3), and the consciousness of utter dependence on God for existence itself that is the nature of all created things (4:11). These most elemental forms of perception of God not only require expression in worship: they cannot be truly experienced except as worship.

The vision mixes cultic and political imagery. Cultic imagery is prominent because the throne-room is the heavenly sanctuary (later explicitly so: 11:19; 15:5–8), prototype of the earthly temple. The living creatures (who combine the features of Isaiah's seraphim [Isa. 6:2] and Ezekiel's cherubim [Ezek. 1:5–14]) are the heavenly prototypes of the two cherubim who flanked the mercy-seat in the holy of holies in the earthly temple (Exod. 25:18–22). They are heavenly beings whose existence is entirely fulfilled in the worship of God. Their ceaseless worship at the heart of all reality, around the divine throne, represents the theocentric nature of all reality, which exists ultimately to glorify God. They are therefore the central worshippers whose worship is taken up by wider circles. These wider circles expand – through chapters 4 and 5 – to include all creatures in the whole cosmos (5:13). In this worship of God and the Lamb by the whole creation (5:13) the eschatological goal of God's purpose for his creation is already anticipated. Appropriately, therefore, the living creatures, who continually express creation's worship with this goal in view, join their own 'Amen!' to it when the goal is reached (5:14).

It is worth noticing how far from anthropocentric is this vision of worship. Humanity is radically displaced from the centre of things where human beings naturally tend to place themselves. At its heart and in its eschatological goal the creation is theocentric, orientated in worship towards its Creator. But even among the worshippers human beings are not pre-eminent. The four living creatures who lead the worship of the whole creation are not portrayed as anthropomorphic beings, as angelic beings often are. Only the third has a face resembling a human face. The others resemble a lion, an ox and an eagle, and with their six wings and myriad eyes all have a heavenly superiority to all earthly creatures (4:6–8). Their representative function is to worship on behalf of all

creatures, and therefore it is fulfilled when the circle of worship
expands to include not only humans, but 'every creature in
heaven and on earth and under the earth and in the sea' (5:13).

As well as cultic imagery, there is political imagery. The
throne-room is the place from which God exercises his rule over
the world. The twenty-four 'elders' – a political, rather than
cultic term – are the angelic beings who compose the divine
council (cf. Isa. 24:23; Dan. 7:9; 2 Enoch 4:1; T. Levi 3:8). As
their own thrones and crowns indicate (4:4), they are themselves rulers. They rule the heavenly world on God's behalf.
They too worship, but significantly they do so by an act of
obeisance in which they get down from their thrones, remove
their crowns and lay them before the divine throne (4:10).
Thus they acknowledge that, as created beings (4:11), their
authority is wholly derivative from God's. He alone is to be
worshipped as the source of all power and authority.

The combination of cultic and political images to portray
God as the acknowledged source and goal of all things was
already traditional in apocalyptic visions of God. But it also
corresponds significantly to the religio–political context of
Revelation. The Roman Empire, like most political powers in
the ancient world, represented and propagated its power in
religious terms. Its state religion, featuring the worship both of
the deified emperors and of the traditional gods of Rome,
expressed political loyalty through religious worship. In this
way it absolutized its power, claiming for itself the ultimate,
divine sovereignty over the world. And so in effect it contested
on earth the divine sovereignty which John sees acknowledged
in heaven in chapter 4. The coming of God's kingdom on earth
must therefore be the replacement of Rome's pretended divine
sovereignty by the true divine sovereignty of the One who sits
on the heavenly throne. Significantly, this conflict of sovereignties is often portrayed in the rest of Revelation by references to
worship. Rome's usurpation of divine rule is indicated by the
universal worship of the beast (e.g. 13:4, 8, 12), whereas the
coming of God's kingdom is indicated by universal worship of
God (15:4; cf. 19:5–6). In the conflict of sovereignties the lines
are drawn between those who worship the beast and those who

worship God. Every stage of God's victory – through chapters
7–19 – is accompanied by worship in heaven. The issue of true
and false worship is fundamental to John's prophetic insight
into the power-structures of the world his readers lived in. In
the end, the book is about the incompatibility of the exclusive
monotheistic worship portrayed in chapter 4 with every kind of
idolatry – the political, social and economic idolatries from
which more narrowly religious idolatry is inseparable.

THE CRITIQUE OF ROMAN POWER

We have indicated how the vision of God in chapter 4 corre-
lates with the religio–political context John addresses in Revelation. It will be useful at this point to interrupt our discussion
of chapter 4 in order briefly to sketch that context as Revelation portrays it. The theology of Revelation is highly contextual. The question of who God is, which the vision of
chapter 4 addresses, related very closely to the world in which
John's readers lived. This is not to say that the context determines the understanding of God, because one could equally
well say that it is the understanding of God which determines
the way John, as a prophet, perceives the context. But we need
to understand the correlation between the understanding of
God in Revelation and Revelation's critique of Roman power
if we are fully to understand both.

Our question is how John, with prophetic insight, perceives
the Roman Empire. Revelation itself allows no neutral perception: either one shares Rome's own ideology, the view of the
Empire promoted by Roman propaganda, or one sees it from
the perspective of heaven, which unmasks the pretensions of
Rome. Revelation portrays the Roman Empire as a system of
violent oppression, founded on conquest, maintained by violence and oppression. It is a system both of political tyranny
and of economic exploitation. The two major symbols for
Rome, which represent different aspects of the empire, are the
sea-monster ('the beast': especially chapters 13 and 17) and the
harlot of Babylon (especially chapters 17–18). The beast represents the military and political power of the Roman Emperors.

Babylon is the city of Rome, in all her prosperity gained by
economic exploitation of the Empire. Thus the critique in
chapter 13 is primarily political, the critique in chapters 17–18
primarily economic, but in both cases also deeply religious.
The beast and the harlot are intimately related. The harlot
rides on the beast (17:3), because the prosperity of the city of
Rome at the Empire's expense and her corrupting influence
over the Empire rest on the power achieved and maintained by
the imperial armies.

Although the Empire is a system of tyranny and exploitation,
John is entirely aware that it was not resisted or opposed by
most of its subjects. In the great cities of the province of Asia,
for example, which John knew well, many were enthusiastic
about Roman rule. This was partly because some provincials
personally benefited from the Empire. In Revelation's terminology, these were especially 'the kings of the earth', that is, the
local ruling classes whom Rome co-opted to participation in
her rule and whose own privileged position in society was
thereby bolstered, and 'the merchants of the earth', who
profited from Rome's economic prosperity. But more generally, Rome's subjects were persuaded to accept and to
welcome her rule by the ideology of the Empire, which John
effectively portrays in two different aspects corresponding to
the beast and the harlot. To take the latter first, although the
harlot lives well at her clients' expense, she also offers them
something (17:4) – the supposed benefits of Roman rule. This is
no doubt the ideology of the *pax Romana*,[5] vigorously promoted
throughout the first century AD, according to which Rome's
gift to the world was the peace and security Rome provided
within the borders of her empire and thereby the conditions of
the Empire's prosperity. Rome, the self-proclaimed eternal
city, offered security to her subjects, and her own dazzling
wealth seemed a prosperity in which her subjects could share.
But Revelation portrays this ideology as a deceitful illusion. It
is the wine with which the harlot intoxicates the nations,
offered in the cup whose exterior is golden, but which contains

---

[5] Cf. K. Wengst, *Pax Romana and the Peace of Jesus Christ* (London: SCM Press, 1987),
part 1.

abominations (17:2, 4). The spurious attraction of the Roman ideology it is one of the purposes of John's prophecy to expose.[6]

The other aspect of the ideology, portrayed in chapter 13, is the worship of power. In 13:3–4, the beast receives a mortal wound in one of its seven heads, but the wound is healed, to the amazement of the people of the world: 'They worshipped the dragon, for he had given his authority to the beast, and they worshipped the beast, saying, "Who is like the beast, and who can fight against it?"' The wounded head of the beast is the emperor Nero, who committed suicide with a sword (cf. 13:14).[7] This wound to a head of the beast was also a mortal wound to the beast itself (the imperial power), and it is the beast which recovers. The allusion is to the events immediately before and after the death of Nero in which it seemed likely that the Empire itself might disintegrate. To many of his subjects Nero's tyranny was obvious and hated: in his case the true nature of the beast became more apparent than usual. Towards the end of Nero's reign there were serious revolts in the provinces. His death was followed by the chaotic 'year of the four emperors'. But the imperial power recovered with the Flavian dynasty. From the brink of collapse it emerged as apparently invincible, so that, according to the vision, the whole world cried, 'Who is like the beast, and who can fight against it?' The words are a parody of the celebration of God's power in the Song of Moses (Exod. 15:11: 'Who is like you, O LORD?'). They point to the absolutizing of political and military power which was expressed in the worship of Rome and the Roman emperors.

In chapter 13 John recognizes two sides to the imperial cult. On the one hand, the beast blasphemes: it gives itself divine names and claims divinity (13:1, 5). In other words, it absolutizes itself by claiming the religious loyalty due only to the ultimate power of God. But John also recognizes that the imperial cult was not imposed on unwilling subjects. It was the

---

[6] On this paragraph, see R. Bauckham, 'The Economic Critique of Rome in Revelation 18', in L. Alexander, ed., *Images of Empire* (*JSOT*SS 122; Sheffield: *JSOT* Press, 1991), 47–90, which becomes chapter 10 in Bauckham, *The Climax of Prophecy*.

[7] See Chapter 11 ('Nero and the Beast') in Bauckham, *The Climax of Prophecy*.

spontaneous response of Rome's subjects to her apparently invincible power (13:3–4). The second beast or earth-monster (13:11), elsewhere in Revelation called the false prophet (16:13; 19:20), who promotes the imperial cult by setting up the image of the beast, giving it godlike characteristics, and enforcing its worship, probably represents the imperial priesthood in the cities of the province of Asia. The imperial cult in these cities originated from the initiative of the cities themselves. But from John's prophetic viewpoint it was dangerous idolatry nonetheless, because it deified political and military power. The imagery of 13:16–17, restricting all economic transactions to those who are certified as worshippers of the beast, is no doubt deliberately exaggerated beyond current practice, in order to highlight the totalitarian direction in which the logic of the absolutizing of power in political religion points.

Thus it is a serious mistake to suppose that Revelation opposes the Roman Empire solely because of its persecution of Christians. Rather Revelation advances a thorough-going prophetic critique of the system of Roman power. It is a critique which makes Revelation the most powerful piece of political resistance literature from the period of the early Empire. It is not simply because Rome persecutes Christians that Christians must oppose Rome. Rather it is because Christians must dissociate themselves from the evil of the Roman system that they are likely to suffer persecution. In fact, the full-scale persecution of the church which John foresees was not yet happening when he wrote. Though there had been martyrdoms (2:13; 6:9–10; 16:6; 17:6), it is clear from the seven messages to the churches that persecution was only sporadic and local. But John sees that the nature of Roman power is such that, if Christians are faithful witnesses to God, then they must suffer the inevitable clash between Rome's divine pretensions and their witness to the true God.

From John's prophetic perspective Rome's evil lay primarily in absolutizing her own power and prosperity. Consequently she pursued and maintained them at the expense of her victims. According to 18:24, it is not just for the martyrdom of

Christians, but for the slaughter of all her innocent victims that Rome will be judged: 'in her was found the blood of prophets and saints, and of all who have been slain on earth'. There is therefore a sense in which Revelation takes a view from the 'underside of history', from the perspective of the victims of Rome's power and glory. It takes this perspective not because John and his Christian readers necessarily belonged to the classes which suffered rather than shared Rome's power and prosperity. It takes this perspective because, if they are faithful in their witness to the true God, their opposition to Rome's oppression and their dissociation of themselves from Rome's evil will make them victims of Rome in solidarity with the other victims of Rome. The special significance of Christian martyrdom is that it makes the issue clear. Those who bear witness to the one true God, the only true absolute, to whom all political power is subject, expose Rome's idolatrous self-deification for what it is.

This means that the power of resistance to Rome came from Christian faith in the one true God. Not to submit to Roman power, not to glorify its violence and its profits, required a perspective alternative to the Roman ideology which permeated public life. For John and those who shared his prophetic insight, it was the Christian vision of the incomparable God, exalted above all worldly power, which relativized Roman power and exposed Rome's pretensions to divinity as a dangerous delusion. This is why the critique of Rome in Revelation follows, in the structure of the book, from the vision of God's rule and justice in chapter 4. In the light of God's righteousness Rome's oppression and exploitation stand condemned, and in the light of God's lordship over history, it becomes clear that Rome does not hold ultimate power and cannot continue her unjust rule indefinitely. Thus, if there is a sense in which Revelation adopts a perspective from the 'underside of history', it is the heavenly perspective, given in the vision of God's heavenly throne-room, that makes this possible.

DIVINE HOLINESS IN JUDGMENT

The whole of Revelation could be regarded as a vision of the
fulfilment of the first three petitions of the Lord's Prayer: 'Your
name be hallowed, your kingdom come, your will be done, on
earth as it is in heaven' (Matt. 6:9–10). John and his readers
lived in a world in which God's name was not hallowed, his
will was not done, and evil ruled through the oppression and
exploitation of the Roman system of power. But in chapter 4,
he sees in heaven, the sphere of ultimate reality, the absolute
holiness, righteousness and sovereignty of God. From this
vision of God's name hallowed and God's will done in heaven,
it follows that his kingdom must come on earth. This is what
makes the vision of chapter 4, along with its christological
continuation in chapter 5, foundational for all that follows. A
wide range of literary and thematic connexions link chapter 4
with the visions that follow. In particular they link chapter 4
with the visions of judgment on the world and the powers of
evil. The holiness and righteousness of God require the condemnation of unrighteousness on earth and the destruction of
the powers of evil that contest God's rule on earth, so that their
rule may give place to the coming of God's kingdom on earth.

There are three series of judgments: the seven seal-openings
(6:1–17; 8:1, 3–5), the seven trumpets (8:2, 6–21; 11:14–19),
and the seven bowls (15:1, 5–21). As seven is the number of
completeness, in some sense each series completes God's judgment on the unrighteous world. In other words, the seventh of
each series portrays the final act of judgment in which evil is
destroyed and God's kingdom arrives. But the three series are
so connected that the seventh seal-opening includes the seven
trumpets and the seventh trumpet includes the seven bowls.
Thus each series reaches the same end, but from starting-points
progressively closer to the end. This is why the three series of
judgments are of progressive severity: the judgments of the
seal-openings affect a quarter of the earth (6:8), those of the
trumpets affect a third (8:7–12; 9:18), but those of the bowls
are unlimited. Warning judgments, restrained in hope that the
wicked will be warned and repent (cf. 9:20–1), are succeeded

in the last series by judgments of final retribution (cf. 16:5–7). Of course, the highly schematized portrayal of the judgments depicts their theological significance. It cannot be meant as a literal prediction of events.

What is of interest to us at present is the way these series of judgments are connected with the vision of God's throne-room in chapter 4. Each series is portrayed as in some way issuing from the throne-room. It is the four living creatures who summon the four riders of the first four seal-openings (6:1, 3, 5, 7). The seven trumpets are blown by the seven angels who stand before God in heaven (8:2, 6). Most elaborate is the way the seven last plagues, with which 'the wrath of God is ended' (15:1), are portrayed as issuing from the throne-room depicted in chapter 4. The heavenly temple is open (15:5); the angels who are to pour out the bowls of wrath on the earth come out of it (15:6); and one of the living creatures gives them the 'bowls full of the wrath of God, who lives for ever and ever' (15:7). This last phrase is an allusion to the way God is described in 4:9–10 (cf. also 10:6). He is the only eternal one: evil must perish under his judgment. Finally, in 15:8 ('the temple was filled with smoke from the glory of God and from his power, and no one could enter the temple until the seven plagues ... were ended') there is an echo of Isaiah 6:4 ('the house filled with smoke'). This completes an allusion to Isaiah's vision of God on his throne which began in chapter 4 with the song of the living creatures (4:8: 'Holy, holy, holy, the Lord God the Almighty', echoing Isaiah 6:3). It is the God whose awesome holiness the living creatures sing unceasingly who manifests his glory and power in the final series of judgments.

Even more significant, however, is the literary link between 4:5a and the seventh of each series of judgments. In 4:5a ('coming from the throne are flashes of lightning and rumblings and peals of thunder') John has developed a feature of Ezekiel's vision of the divine throne (Ezek. 1:13) into an allusion to the phenomena of the thunderstorm that accompanied God's self-manifestation on Mount Sinai (Exod. 19:16; 20:18). This feature of John's vision therefore represents the One who sits on the throne as the holy God of the Sinai covenant, who demands obedience to his righteous will. But the formula used in 4:5a is then echoed at the opening of the seventh seal (8:5), the sounding of the seventh trumpet (11:19) and the pouring out of the seventh bowl (16:18–21), in the following way:

4:5:   'flashes of lightning and rumblings and peals of thunder'
8:5:   'peals of thunder, rumblings, flashes of lightning, and an earthquake'
11:19:   'flashes of lightning, rumblings, peals of thunders, an earthquake, and heavy hail'
16:18–21:   'flashes of lightning, rumblings, peals of thunder, and a violent earthquake ... and huge hailstones'

In 4:5 the formula indicates a manifestation of God's holiness in heaven. The expansion of the formula in the other instances indicates that judgment on earth is now in view (as the context of each makes quite clear). God's holiness is manifested in judgment on evil. The progressive expansion of the formula corresponds to the progressive intensification of the three series of judgments. In this way the whole course of the judgments is depicted as the manifestation of the same divine holiness which is revealed in the theophany in heaven in 4:5.

In all these connexions between the vision of God's throne in chapter 4 and the three series of judgments it is notable that the transcendence of God is protected and the absence of anthropomorphic representation, so notable a feature of chapter 4, is preserved. God is not directly depicted as judge. The living creatures who belong to God's throne (4:6) commission the judgments (6:1, 3, 5, 7; 15:7) and angels carry them out. God's glory, power and holiness are manifested in smoke, thunderstorm and earthquake – the traditional accompaniments of theophany – but God himself is not seen or heard. Even when John refers to the great voice, which at the pouring out of the seventh bowl declares the completion of the judgment ('It is done'), he adopts the kind of indirectness with which Jewish writers commonly avoided the anthropomorphism of reference to God's own voice. The voice is not said to be God's, but comes 'from the throne' (16:17). Thus the way John portrays the judgments is as far as possible from the image of a human despot wielding arbitrary power.

This point is of the greatest importance when we remember that John's purpose is certainly not to compare the divine sovereignty in heaven with the absolute power of human rulers on earth. Quite the contrary: his purpose is to oppose the two. Absolute power on earth is satanic in inspiration, destructive in its effects, idolatrous in its claim to ultimate loyalty. Though it claims divinity, it is utterly unlike the divine sovereignty. Thus it would subvert the whole purpose of John's prophecy if his depiction of the divine sovereignty appeared to be a projection into heaven of the absolute power claimed by human rulers on earth. This danger is averted by a kind of apophaticism[8] in the imagery which purges it of anthropomorphism and suggests the incomparability of God's sovereignty. His judgments are true and just (16:7; 19:2; cf. 15:3). In other words, they correspond to the moral truth of things. He is sovereign as the only holy One (15:4). In other words, he alone has righteousness as his very nature. The absolute sovereignty which should be attributed to the Creator, the source of all value, who is truth and righteousness in his very being, is not at all the same thing as the absolute sovereignty claimed by finite creatures on earth. No writer of Scripture shows himself more aware of this difference than John.

DIVINE SOVEREIGNTY AND TRANSCENDENCE

The image of God as transcendent ruler and judge has been frequently and severely criticized in much recent theological discussion. Feminist theologians have not been alone in rejecting it, but have often been particularly vehement in castigating it as a religious projection of patriarchal domination.[9] This image, as we shall see especially in our next two chapters, does not exhaust Revelation's understanding of God, but it does play a prominent part in that understanding, and so

---

[8] Apophaticism (or negative theology) radically distinguishes God from all creaturely being by conceiving him in negative terms: he is *not* what creatures are.

[9] E.g. D. Hampson, *Theology and Feminism* (Oxford: Blackwell, 1990), 151–3.

it is relevant to ask whether Revelation's use of this image of God would justifiably incur the kinds of criticism that are levelled at it by feminist and other contemporary theologians.

Two types of criticism are worth considering. The first is that images of God as sovereign function as religious sanction for authoritarian structures of power and domination in human society. Of course, this has very often been the case. It is one of the deepest ironies of Christian history that, when the Roman Empire became nominally Christian under the Christian emperors, Christianity came to function not so very differently from the state religion which Revelation portrays as Rome's idolatrous self-deification. The Christian emperor's rule was seen as an image of God's own sovereignty, and while this did include the notion of the emperor's responsibility to God, it also provided religious justification for absolute monarchy. However, this is the exact opposite of the way the image of divine sovereignty functions in Revelation. There, so far from legitimizing human autocracy, divine rule radically de-legitimizes it. Absolute power, by definition, belongs only to God, and it is precisely the recognition of God's absolute power that relativizes all human power. The image of God's sovereignty functioned rather similarly in seventeenth-century England, where it played a part in the religious origins of modern democracy. Because God is king, it was said, all men and women are equally his subjects, and no man should arrogate to himself to rule over his fellows.[10]

We have already noticed how Revelation, by avoiding anthropomorphism, suggests the incomparability of God's sovereignty. In effect, the image of sovereignty is being used to express an aspect of the relation between God and his creatures which is unique, rather than one which provides a model for relationships between humans. Of course, the image of the throne derives from the human world, but it is so used as to highlight the difference, more than the similarity, between divine sovereignty and human sovereignty. In other words, it is

[10] D. Nicholls, *Deity and Domination* (London and New York: Routledge, 1989), 236. (This book is an excellent treatment of this issue in nineteenth- and twentieth-century religious and political thought.)

used to express transcendence. Much of the modern criticism of images of this kind seems unable to understand real transcendence. It supposes that the relation between God and the world must be in every respect comparable with relations between creatures and that all images of God must function as models for human behaviour. It is critical of images of transcendence, such as sovereignty, but it takes transcendence to mean that God is some kind of superhuman being alongside other beings. Real transcendence, of course, means that God transcends all creaturely existence. As the source, ground and goal of all creaturely existence, the infinite mystery on which all finite being depends, his relation to us is unique. We can express it only by using language and images in odd ways that point beyond themselves to something quite incomparable with the creaturely sources of our language and images.

Once we recognize the need for God-language that points to transcendence, we can recognize that John is remarkably successful in finding religiously evocative language that expresses transcendence. His distinctive interpretations of the divine name – the Alpha and the Omega, the One who is and who was and who is to come – attempt to name the one who precedes and surpasses all infinite existence, while being intimately related to it as its source and goal. These designations for God are also notably non-anthropomorphic, suggesting that God's relation to the world transcends human analogies. As for the image of the throne the way John uses it not only evokes transcendence, but does so polemically against the deification of human power. Finally, John's vision draws the reader into worship of the One who alone is holy and who alone is Creator, awaking those forms of perception of God which are the recognition of transcendence. It is in the kind of genuine worship that John portrays in his vision of heaven that we know ourselves to be finite creatures in relation to the transcendent mystery of God. False worship, such as John portrays in the worship of the beast, is false precisely because its object is not the transcendent mystery, but only the mystification of something finite. Hence the capacity of the visions of Revelation to evoke divine transcendence is indispensable to its prophetic purpose of distinguishing true worship from idolatry, the true God from the false.

A second type of criticism of the image of God as sovereign ruler over his creation is that it represents God as distant from the world, rather than involved in and with his creation.[11] This criticism is misconceived when it is made against transcendence as such. Transcendence requires the absolute distinction between God and finite creatures, but not at all his distance from them. The transcendent God, precisely because he is not one finite being among others, is able to be incomparably present to all, closer to them than they are to themselves. This point is relevant to Revelation, because it explains how the God whose transcendence is so emphasized can in the new creation make his home with human beings (21:3). His nearness to his creation in the language of 21:3–4 is as striking as his transcendence in the vision of chapter 4. Moreover, even the image of the throne becomes, in the New Jerusalem, an expression of God's closeness to his people (22:3–4; and cf. already 7:15–17).

We become aware then that the visions portray a difference between the present and the eschatological future. God as the One who sits on the throne is at present in heaven and acts on earth only through angelic intermediaries. Only in God's eschatological coming to his creation at the end, only in the New Jerusalem which comes down out of heaven and abolishes the distinction between heaven and earth, will God's dwelling be with his people on earth. The impression that God is in some sense now absent from the earth is confirmed by the difference between the song of the living creatures (4:8) and the Old Testament original on which it is modelled: Isaiah 6:3. Isaiah's seraphim sing, 'Holy, holy, holy is the LORD of hosts; the whole earth is full of his glory.' In John's vision, the last clause is replaced by the designation of God: 'who was and who is and who is to come'. We recall that chapter 4 portrays in heaven the rule of God which is yet to come on earth. God's glory is not yet manifested in a world dominated by injustice. But this is

<hr>

[11] E.g. S. McFague, *Models of God: Theology for an Ecological, Nuclear Age* (London: SCM Press, 1987), 63–9.

not an other-worldly dualism, which rejects this world in favour of another. It is a recognition of the evil which obscures God's glory in the world as it is, but it is also the hope that, rescued from evil, this world will be indwelt by the splendour of God.

It is part and parcel of the apocalyptic outlook to portray the present and the eschatological future in starkly black and white terms. No doubt most modern Christians would prefer to recognize the traces of God's glory even within a world where human injustice looms large. But Revelation deals in images which cannot say everything at once. The point here is an overwhelming concern with the absence of God's righteousness from God's world, a concern John shares with the Jewish apocalyptic tradition. While the beast holds sway, God cannot be said to be present in his glory. True, even the beast has power only by divine permission (13:7), but only when God's will prevails over all evil can his kingdom be said to have come on earth (11:15). Only then will he make his dwelling in his creation (21:3).

Yet, if the One who sits on the throne is in some sense removed from the world in heaven, Revelation does portray God's presence in the world as presently dominated by evil. As we shall see in the next two chapters, the image of the Lamb represents God's sacrificial, suffering involvement in the world and the Spirit his presence in the church's sacrificial witness to the truth.

GOD THE CREATOR

We have considered at length the sovereignty of God portrayed in chapter 4. Equally important, and closely connected, is the confession of God as Creator, expressed in the hymn of the twenty-four elders:

> You are worthy, our Lord and God,
>> to receive glory and honour and power,
> for you created all things,
>> and by your will they existed and were created.

This is the understanding of God as Creator which was characteristic of Judaism and which early Christianity shared without question. The one God is defined as the One who brought all things into existence. As Creator, he alone has ultimate power over everything. As Creator, to whom all creatures owe their very being, he alone is to be worshipped. As this chapter of Revelation itself illustrates, Jewish monotheism was not compromised by the common belief in a multitude of other heavenly beings, because, as the elders here confess, they are emphatically creatures, owing their existence to God. Jewish monotheism in New Testament times was defined by the doctrine of creation and by the practice of worship. The one Creator of all things is God and he alone may be worshipped.

Consequently, when an angel proclaims the 'eternal gospel' to all people on earth, calling them to repentance in view of the imminent final judgment, the substance of this gospel is a call to recognize their Creator by worshipping him: 'Fear God and give him glory, for the hour of his judgment has come; and worship him who made heaven and earth, the sea and the springs of water' (14:7). The worship which the whole earth is giving to the beast (13:8) is really due to God, because he, not the beast, is the Creator of all things.

The understanding of God as Creator was not only integral to Jewish and Christian monotheism; it was also essential to the development of Jewish and Christian eschatology. If God was the transcendent source of all things, he could also be the source of quite new possibilities for his creation in the future. Creation is not confined for ever to its own immanent possibilities. It is open to the fresh creative possibilities of its Creator. This is how the hope of resurrection was possible. The Jewish hope of resurrection was not based on belief in the inherent capacity of human nature to survive death (although some kind of survival was often assumed). It was fundamentally a form of trust in God the Creator, who, as he gave the life that ends in death, can also give life back to the dead. More than that, he can give *new* life – eschatologically new life raised forever beyond the threat of death. Whereas mortal life, cut off from its source, ends in death, God can give new life which is so united to his own eternal life that it can share his own eternity.[12]

But Jewish eschatological hope was not just for the resurrection of individuals. It was hope for the future of God's whole creation. It was hope for *new* creation (cf. 1 Enoch 72:1; 91:16; 2 Bar. 44:12; *L.A.B.* 3:10; 2 Pet. 3:13, all inspired by Isa. 65:17; 66:22). This did not mean the replacement of this creation by another, as we can see from parallel references to the *renewal* of the creation (Jub. 1:29; 2 Bar. 32:6; 4 Ezra 7:75; cf. 1 Enoch 45:5). Revelation 21:1, which directly echoes the language of Isaiah (43:18–19; 65:17), belongs among those passages which might at first sight be thought to suggest the replacement of this creation by a wholly different one:

Then I saw a new heaven and a new earth; for the first heaven and the first earth had passed away ...

The words 'first' and 'new' here carry their almost technical apocalyptic reference to the contrast between, on the one hand, the creation of the present age which is passing away, and, on the other hand, the *eschatologically* new, that is, the qualitatively quite different life of the eternal age to come. The discontinuity is parallel, on a cosmic scale, to the discontinuity, in the case of human persons, between this mortal life and the eschatologically new life of resurrection. The first creation, by its nature, lapses back into nothing. It requires a fresh creative act of God to give it, as it were, a quite new form of existence, taken beyond all threat of evil and destruction, indwelt by his own glory, participating in his own eternity. As 21:4 makes clear, it is the end of suffering and mortality that is in mind when Revelation speaks of the 'passing away' of 'the first things'. That the contrast between 'the first heaven and the first earth', on the one hand, and 'the new heaven and the new earth', on the other, refers to the eschatological renewal of this creation, not its replacement by another, is further confirmed

---

[12] On this paragraph, see R. Bauckham, 'God Who Raises the Dead: The Resurrection of Jesus in Relation to Early Christian Faith in God', forthcoming in P. Avis, ed., *The Resurrection of Jesus Christ* (Edinburgh: T. & T. Clark).

by the observation that Jewish and Christian writers could speak rather similarly of the earth that perished in the Flood and the new world that emerged from the Flood (cf. 2 Pet. 3:6), understanding the Flood as a reversion of creation to the chaos from which it was first created. We shall return to the parallel with the Flood shortly.

In 21:5, for the first and only time since 1:8, the One who sits on the throne speaks directly. He makes the solemn declaration, 'Behold, I make all things new.' The key significance of the words, which echo Isaiah 65:17 (cf. 43:19), is underlined by God's own command to John to write them, which follows. They correspond to 4:11: 'you created all things'. The universality of the eschatological new beginning corresponds to the derivation of all things from God's original creative act. This connection between creation and new creation highlights the cosmic scope of John's theological horizon, within which his primary concern with the human world is set.

The full meaning of the biblical understanding of creation, that the whole of finite reality exists only by God the Creator's gift of existence, has become suspect within the same currents of contemporary theology as are critical of the image of sovereignty.[13] In part, this represents a distaste for the wholly asymmetrical relationship of the absolute dependence of the creation on the will of the Creator, in favour of some kind of mutuality between God and creation. But the theology of Revelation may help us to recognize two inevitable effects of such tendencies. In the first place, they betray one of the roots of the religious apprehension of the uniqueness of God: the awareness that beyond all the interdependence of creation, there is One to whom alone all things owe even existence (and therefore everything). This awareness is inseparable from monotheistic worship, in which worship is acknowledgment of the ultimacy and incomparability of this Creator and is therefore not given to any finite beings, which in the last resort are fellow-creatures of the same Creator (cf. Rev. 19:9–10; 22:8–9).

---

[13] E.g. D. Hampson, *Theology and Feminism* (Oxford: Blackwell, 1990), 131–2; S. McFague, *Models of God: Theology for an Ecological, Nuclear Age* (London: SCM Press, 1987), 109–10.

Such awareness and worship (expressed in 4:11) by no means contradict or diminish the relative independence and significant creativity of creatures themselves, nor relationships of real mutuality between God and creation, but they go behind these things to acknowledge that they too are *given* by the Creator.

Secondly, reducing the real transcendence of the Creator reduces the openness of his creation to the eschatologically new. A God who is not the transcendent origin of all things but a way of speaking of the immanent creative possibilities of the universe itself cannot be the ground of ultimate hope for the future of creation. Where faith in God the Creator wanes, so inevitably does hope for resurrection, let alone the new creation of all things. It is the God who is the Alpha who will also be the Omega.

THE CREATOR'S FAITHFULNESS TO CREATION

The eschatological hope of Revelation actually has its basis, not only in the understanding of God as Creator, but also in the belief in the Creator's faithfulness to his creation. If faith in God as Creator raises the possibility of new creation, it is trust in his faithfulness to his creation which gives hope for new creation. This faithfulness of the Creator to his creation is the theological subject of the Flood narrative in Genesis and was expressed in the covenant with Noah (usually so called, but actually, according to Genesis, God's covenant with Noah and all creation). There is probably an allusion to the Noahic covenant in Revelation 4:3. Although the rainbow round the throne was certainly suggested by Ezekiel's vision of the divine throne, in which the splendour of the figure on the throne was said to be like a rainbow (Ezek. 1:28), it is likely that, just as John found a hint of the Sinai theophany in the lightning of Ezekiel's vision (Ezek. 1:13; Rev. 4;5), so he saw in Ezekiel's allusion to the rainbow the sign of the covenant with Noah. Thus, whereas Ezekiel described the divine splendour as '*like* the appearance of a rainbow', John sees around the throne 'a rainbow like an emerald in appearance'. The rainbow moves

from simile to reality as it becomes the bow that God set in the
heavens after the Flood as a sign of his covenant with the earth
(Gen. 9:13–17).

The extent to which the Creator's faithfulness to his creation
is the theme of Revelation can be appreciated if we notice a
significant allusion to the Genesis Flood story in Revelation
11:18. The time of the end – the judgment and the inauguration of God's kingdom – is there said to be, among other
things, the time 'for destroying the destroyers of the earth'.
This is an example of the eschatological *jus talionis*, a way of
speaking of God's eschatological judgment in which the
description of the punishment matches verbally the description
of the sin (cf. other examples in 16:6; 18:6; 22:18–19). It was a
literary way of indicating the absolute justice of God's judgment: the punishment matches the crime. In this case, the
verbal correspondence is achieved by the use of a Greek verb
(*diaphtheirō*) which can mean both 'destroy', in the sense of
causing to perish, and 'ruin', in the sense of corrupting with
evil.[14] The 'destroyers of the earth' are the powers of evil: the
dragon, the beast, and the harlot of Babylon (who in 19:2 is
said to have 'corrupted – or destroyed – the earth with her
fornication'). With their violence, oppression and idolatrous
religion they are ruining God's creation. His faithfulness to his
creation requires that he destroy them in order to preserve and
to deliver it from evil.

However, the phrase – 'for destroying the destroyers of the
earth' – also alludes to the equivalent wordplay in Genesis
6:11–13, 17, where the Hebrew verb *šāḥat* has the same double
meaning. God there determines to *destroy*, along with the earth
itself, those who are *corrupting* the earth with their evil ways.
This he did in the Flood, which was a divine judgment aimed
at delivering God's creation from the ruinous violence of its
inhabitants.

At first sight, this parallel between the Flood and the eschatological judgment to which Revelation 11:18 refers might
seem to contradict the covenant with Noah, rather than indi-

---

[14] Cf. a similar use of *phtheirō* in another sentence of eschatological *jus talionis:* 1 Cor.
3:17.

cating God's faithfulness to it. In that covenant, God promised that 'never again shall there be a flood to destroy the earth' (Gen. 9:11). However, we should remember the way in which the earth was destroyed in the Flood. The waters of the flood are understood as the primeval waters of chaos or the waters of the abyss (Gen. 1:2; 7:11), which God in creation had restrained and held at bay, but had not abolished (Gen. 1:6–7). They symbolize the power of nothingness to undo creation, a destructive potential which remains to threaten the created universe with reversion to chaos. In the narrative of the Flood, God is represented as allowing the waters of the abyss to flood the world, returning it to chaos (cf. 1 Enoch 83:4).

These waters of chaos are the sea from which the beast, with his destructive violence, arises (Rev. 13:1; cf. Dan. 7:2–3). At the parousia the beast himself is removed (19:20), but not yet the potentiality for evil. Following the destruction of the devil, death and Hades (20:10, 14) – the last of the destroyers of the earth – the new creation is characterized by one feature that makes it really, eschatologically new: 'the sea was no more' (21:1). The waters of the primeval abyss, that represent the source of destructive evil, the possibility of the reversion of creation to chaos, are finally no more. So the judgment of the old creation and the inauguration of the new is not so much a second Flood as the final removal of the threat of another Flood. In new creation God makes his creation eternally secure from any threat of destructive evil. In this way Revelation portrays God as faithful to the Noahic covenant and indeed surpassing it in his faithfulness to his creation: first by destroying the destroyers of the earth, finally by taking creation beyond the threat of evil. Only then does it become the home he indwells with the splendour of his divine glory (21:3, 22, 23).

CHAPTER 3

The Lamb on the throne

Christian dogmatics has traditionally distinguished, as two doctrinal topics, the person of Christ and the work of Christ. Although the two are, of course, closely connected, we shall make use of the distinction, in order to study, in the present chapter, Revelation's identification of Jesus Christ with God, and in the next chapter, its understanding of Jesus Christ's work of establishing God's kingdom on earth.

THE FIRST AND THE LAST

John's vision begins with a Christophany. The risen Christ appears as a glorious heavenly being (1:12–16), and declares his identity thus:

I am the first and the last, and the living one. I was dead, and see, I am alive forever and ever; and I have the keys of Death and Hades.
(1:17–18)

In the last chapter we have already noticed that the self-declaration, 'I am the first and the last', corresponds to the divine self-declaration, 'I am the Alpha and Omega' (1:8), and that in Revelation as a whole there is the following pattern of two self-declarations by God and two by Christ:

God: I am the Alpha and the Omega.
(1:8)

Christ: I am the first and the last.
(1:17)

God: I am the Alpha and the Omega, the beginning and the end.
(21:6)

54

Christ: I am the Alpha and the Omega, the first and the last, the
beginning and the end.

(22:13)

A close study of this pattern can reveal the remarkable extent
to which Revelation identifies Jesus Christ with God.

As we have seen, the two titles, 'the Alpha and the Omega',
'the beginning and the end', used of God, designate God as
eternal in relation to the world. He precedes and originates all
things, as their Creator, and he will bring all things to their
eschatological fulfilment. The titles cannot mean anything else
when they are used of Christ in 22:13. Although it might initially seem that God and Christ are in some way distinguished
by the two different self-declarations in 1:8 and 1:17, in 22:13
the placing of the title which is used only of Christ ('the first and
the last') between those which have hitherto been used only of
God seems deliberately to align all three as equivalent.
Moreover, since the title, 'the first and the last', is the one that
occurs in divine self-declarations in Deutero-Isaiah (Isa. 44:6;
48:12), with very much the significance that the other two titles
have in Revelation, it would be very odd if precisely this one
meant something different from the others in Revelation.

It has sometimes been argued that its meaning is different.
Its context in the first part of John's vision, which concerns
Christ's relationship with the seven churches, and its connexion with the resurrection in 1:17–18, a connexion repeated in
2:8, could suggest that it refers to Christ, not as first and last in
relation to all creation, but as first and last in relation to the
church. As 'firstborn from the dead' (1:5), the risen Christ is
the origin of the church, which he will also bring to fulfilment
in his parousia. However, this is not the only way to read
1:17–18. The declaration begins by asserting Christ's participation in the eternal being of God, the origin and goal of all
things ('I am the first and the last'), and then continues by
asserting the particular – indeed, extraordinary – way in which
he, as 'the living one' (1:18), shares God's eternal livingness.
Whereas of God it is said that he is 'the One who is and who
was and who is to come' (1:8) or that he is 'the One who lives
forever and ever' (4:9, 10; 10:6; 15:7), Christ says: 'I was dead,

and behold, I am alive forever and ever' (1:18). His eternal livingness was interrupted by the experience of a human death, and he shares the eternal life of God through triumph over death. Therefore also, whereas the divine self-declaration in 1:8 states the divine lordship as his power over all things, the corresponding statement of Christ's participation in the divine lordship in 1:18 refers to the authority over death and Hades which he has won through his death and resurrection: 'I have the keys of Death and Hades.'

The derivation of the title, 'the first and the last', from Deutero-Isaiah, and the way it is used in 22:13, make this interpretation of 1:17–18 the preferable one. That a reference to Christ's participation in God's creation of all things is not out of place in the context of his address to the churches is clear from 3:14, where the beginning of the message to the church at Laodicea calls him: 'the origin (*archē*) of God's creation'. This does not mean that he was the first created being or that in his resurrection he was the beginning of God's new creation. It must have the same sense as the first part of the title, 'the beginning (*archē*) and the end', as used of both God (21:6) and Christ (22:13). Christ preceded all things as their source. In this belief in Christ's role in creation, Revelation is at one with the Pauline literature (1 Cor. 8:6; Col. 1:15–17), Hebrews (1:2) and the Fourth Gospel (1:1–3). The belief came about through an identification of Christ with the Word or the Wisdom of God through which God created the world, and this identification can be clearly seen in the way Christ's role in creation is expressed in the references outside Revelation just given.[1] In Revelation it has been brought together with another, probably even earlier, christological development of the early church: the identification of God's eschatological coming with the expected parousia of Jesus Christ. These two developments have the effect, then, of including Christ as divine agent both in God's creation of all things and in God's eschatological fulfilment of all things. Thus Christ is 'the Alpha and the Omega, the first and the last, the beginning and the end'. As a

[1] See J. D. G. Dunn, *Christology in the Making* (London: SCM Press, 1980), chapters VI–VII; J. F. Balchin, 'Paul, Wisdom and Christ', in H. H. Rowdon, ed., *Christ the Lord: Studies in Christology presented to Donald Guthrie* (Leicester: Inter-Varsity Press, 1982), 204 19.

way of stating unambiguously that Jesus Christ belongs to the fullness of the eternal being of God, this surpasses anything in the New Testament.

The point can be reinforced by a closer consideration of the pattern formed by the four passages (1:8, 17; 21:6; 22:13) in which these three titles are used as self-designations by God and Christ. In the structure of the book, John's vision (1:9–22:9) is framed by a prologue (1:1–8) and an epilogue (22:6–21: the end of the vision and the beginning of the epilogue overlap, so that 22:6–9 belongs to both). There are a number of literary ways in which the prologue and the epilogue correspond. One of these is that the divine self-designation at the end of the prologue (1:8) corresponds to the self-designation by Christ near the beginning of the epilogue (22:13). These two verses correspond further in that each is preceded by an announcement of the parousia (1:7: 'Behold, he is coming ... '; 22:12: 'Behold, I am coming ... '). If 1:8 and 22:13 correspond in this way, 1:17 and 21:6, placed respectively towards the beginning and towards the end of the vision, also correspond, so that the four texts form a chiastic arrangement (A–B–B¹–A¹). There is, further, a certain thematic resemblance between 1:17 and 21:6 in that in both cases the one who declares himself 'the first and the last' or 'the Alpha and the Omega' also declares himself the source of new, eschatological life: Christ through his resurrection (1:18), God through his new creation of all things and his gift of the water of life (21:1–6).

The chiastic pattern can be set out as follows:

A	B	B¹	A¹
1:8	1:17	21:6	22:13
end of prologue	beginning of vision	end of vision	beginning of epilogue
God	Christ	God	Christ
Alpha and Omega		Alpha and Omega	Alpha and Omega
	first and last		first and last
		beginning and end	beginning and end
connexion with parousia (1:7)	connexion with new life (1:18)	connexion with new life (21:5–6)	connexion with parousia (22:12)

This pattern underlines the identification of Christ with God
which the use of the titles themselves expresses. It also shows
how, as we might expect, it is with the eschatological thrust of
the titles that John is predominantly concerned. It is in Christ's
parousia that God who is the beginning of all things will also
become the end of all things. It is the eschatological life that
Christ entered at his resurrection which all the redeemed
creation will share in God's new creation. But if the eschatological aspect of the titles shared by God and Christ is the
primary concern of John's work, the protological aspect is also
christologically important. It shows that the identification of
Christ with God implied by the titles is not the result of an
adoptionist Christology, in which the mere man Jesus is
exalted at his resurrection to divine status. Important as the
resurrection is for Christ's participation in God's lordship (cf.
2:28; 3:21), these titles he shares with God indicate that he
shared the eternal being of God from before creation.

In Deutero-Isaiah, the title 'the first and the last' is closely
connected with the exclusive monotheism characteristic of that
prophet's message. Yahweh declares: 'I am the first and the
last; besides me there is no god' (Isa. 44:6). It is therefore the
more remarkable that precisely this title is the one by which
Christ declares his identity in Revelation 1:17. It does not
designate him a second god, but includes him in the eternal
being of the one God of Israel who is the only source and goal
of all things. We shall see that John is careful also in other ways
to preserve Jewish monotheistic faith while also including Jesus
in the deity of the one God.

THE WORSHIP OF JESUS

In our last chapter we have seen how important worship is in
Revelation. It has very precise theological meaning. For
Jewish monotheism it marks the distinction between the one
God the Creator of all things, who must be worshipped, and his
creatures, to worship whom is idolatry. Since it marks this
distinction in religious practice it is a more important indication of the real meaning of Jewish and early Christian

monotheism than are more speculative reflections on the unity of God. The tendency of some modern writers to suppose that what is expressed in worship cannot be taken theologically seriously should be rejected, at least in this context in which the restriction of worship to the one God and the doctrine of creation to which it was closely linked were precisely the points Jewish and Christian writers emphasized in opposing their monotheism to pagan idolatry. The polemical significance of worship is clear in Revelation, which sees the root of the evil of the Roman Empire to lie in the idolatrous worship of merely human power, and therefore draws the lines of conflict between the worshippers of the beast and the worshippers of the one true God. John's high consciousness of the issue of monotheistic worship is further expressed, in the closing chapters of the book, in an incident, included twice for strategic effect, in which John prostrates himself before the angel who mediates the revelation to him.[2] The angel protests that he is no more than a fellow-servant of God and directs John to worship God (19:10; 22:8–9). These passages employ a traditional motif found elsewhere in apocalyptic literature.[3] The heavenly glory and supernatural authority of the angelic beings encountered by apocalyptic visionaries not unnaturally provoke a response bordering on worship, but the principle of monotheistic worship is strongly asserted when even the most exalted heavenly beings reject worship and insist that only God should be worshipped. In the passages in Revelation, the point is that the angel who shows the visions to John is not the source of revelation, but only the instrument for communicating it to John. Jesus, however, is represented as the source of revelation (22:16). The implication would seem to be that he is not, like the angel, excluded from monotheistic worship, but included in it. This implication is confirmed by the explicit worship of Jesus elsewhere in Revelation.

[2] The argument of this and the next three paragraphs is presented in greater detail in R. Bauckham, 'The Worship of Jesus in Apocalyptic Christianity', *NTS* 27 (1980–1), 322–41; revised version: chapter 4 ('The Worship of Jesus'), in Bauckham, *The Climax of Prophecy*.

[3] Ap.Zeph. 6:11–15; Asc.Isa. 7:21–2; 8:5; Ap.Paul (Coptic ending); cf. Tob. 12:16–22; Jos.As. 15:12; Gospel of Pseudo-Matthew 3:3; Lad.Jac. 3:3–5; 3 Enoch 16:2–5.

Since the issue of monotheistic worship is so clear in Revelation, it cannot be that the worship of Jesus is represented in Revelation through neglect of this issue. It seems rather that the worship of Jesus must be understood as indicating the inclusion of Jesus in the being of the one God defined by monotheistic worship. The point becomes clear in the scene of worship in heaven in chapters 4–5. We have seen in our last chapter how the worship of God by the heavenly court in chapter 4 is connected with the acknowledgment of God as the Creator of all things (4:11). In chapter 5 the Lamb, Christ, who has triumphed through his death and resurrection and who is seen standing on the divine throne (the probable meaning of 5:6; cf. 7:17), now becomes in turn the centre of the circle of worship in heaven, receiving the obeisance of the living creatures and the elders (5:8). Then the circle expands and the myriads of angels join the living creatures and the elders in a form of worship (5:12) clearly parallel to that offered to God (4:11). Finally, the circle expands to include the whole of creation in a doxology addressed to God and the Lamb together (5:13). It is important to notice how the scene is so structured that the worship of the Lamb (5:8–12) leads to the worship of God and the Lamb together (5:13). John does not wish to represent Jesus as an alternative object of worship alongside God, but as one who shares in the glory due to God. He is worthy of divine worship because his worship can be included in the worship of the one God.

Probably connected with this concern to include Jesus in *monotheistic* worship is a peculiar grammatical usage elsewhere in Revelation, where mention of God and Christ together is followed by a singular verb (11:15) or singular pronouns (22:3–4; and 6:17, where the singular pronoun *autou* is the better reading). It is not clear whether the singular in these cases refers to God alone or to God and Christ together as a unity. John, who is very sensitive to the theological implications of language and even prepared to defy grammar for the sake of theology (cf. 1:4), may well intend the latter. But in either case, he is evidently reluctant to speak of God and Christ together as a plurality. He never makes them the subjects of a plural verb or uses a plural pronoun to refer to them both. The reason is surely clear: he places Christ on the divine side of the distinction between God and creation, but he wishes to avoid ways of speaking which sound to him polytheistic. The consistency of his usage shows that he has reflected carefully on the relation of Christology to monotheism. It is significant that one of the passages in question (22:3–4) again concerns worship.

In 5:8–14 and 22:3–4 the worship is heavenly and eschatological. The doxology addressed to Christ alone in 1:5b–6, one of three such doxologies in the New Testament (along with 2 Tim. 4:18; 2 Pet. 3:18), shows that John and his churches themselves practised the worship of Jesus. Doxologies, with their confession that glory belongs eternally to the One who is addressed, were a Jewish form of praise to the one God. There could be no clearer way of ascribing to Jesus the worship due to God.

There is good evidence, besides that of Revelation, that the worship of Jesus was part of early Christian religious practice from a relatively early date and that it developed within Jewish Christianity where consciousness of the connexion between monotheism and worship was high.[4] It cannot be attributed to Gentile Christian carelessness of the requirement of monotheistic worship. It must be regarded as a development internal to the tradition of Jewish monotheism, by which Jewish Christians implicitly included Jesus in the reality of the one God. The author of Revelation stands within this Jewish Christian tradition and, still within a thoroughly Jewish framework of thought, has reflected deliberately on the relation of Christology to monotheism. Both in the last section and this, we have seen evidence that he has made a rather sophisticated attempt to use language that includes Jesus in the eternal being of God without stepping outside the Jewish monotheism which for him was axiomatic, not least as part of the prophetic and apocalyptic tradition in which as a prophet he very consciously stands. He does not use the abstract conceptuality with which later

---

[4] R. Bauckham, 'Jesus, Worship of', in D. N. Freedman, ed., *The Anchor Bible Dictionary* (Garden City, New York: Doubleday, 1992) vol. 3, 812–19; L. W. Hurtado, *One God, One Lord* (Philadelphia: Fortress Press, 1988).

Christian theologians, drawing on Greek philosophy, were able to say that the Son of God shares the divine nature of his Father. He does not even use the Jewish concept of the Wisdom of God, with which some other Jewish Christians were able to include Christ in the one divine being. His theological idiom is very different, involving the apocalyptic image of the divine throne, the practice of worship, the careful use of grammar and the literary connexions and structures into which, as a literary artist rather than a philosopher, he has put much of his theological expression. It is probably because his idiom is so different from that of later patristic reflection on Christology that the significance of his work in this respect has rarely been recognized.

In the language of the doxology to Christ (1:5b–6) and of the heavenly hymn to the Lamb, which closely resembles it (5:9–10), we can recognize at least part of the impetus that must originally have led to the worship of Jesus. He is there praised for his work of redemption. It was because Christians owed salvation to Jesus Christ that he was worshipped. An overwhelming religious debt to one who was regarded as living in heaven and indeed an experienced presence in the Christian community was naturally expressed in worship. The salvation was too closely connected with Jesus himself for Jesus to be bypassed in worship offered to God for it, but at the same time it was salvation from God that Jesus gave and so Jesus was not treated as an alternative object of worship alongside God. He was included in worship of God. More generally, we could say that it was because Jesus *functioned* as God in early Christian religion that he was worshipped. All the divine functions in relation to the world – as Saviour, Lord and Judge – were exercised by Jesus, of course on God's behalf. The one who functions as God naturally receives divine worship. Thus it is true that worship of Jesus was connected with the functional divinity which is often said to be the only kind of divinity Jewish Christianity attributed to Jesus. But it is doubtful whether, once Jesus was worshipped, Jewish monotheists could for long be content with merely functional divinity. The one who is worthy of the worship due only to God must somehow belong to the reality of the one God.

Certainly the author of Revelation has reached this thought. Although his account of the relation of Jesus to God remains close to the primary religious concern with God's and Jesus' relation to the world and does not speculate on the being of God apart from the world, the evidence we have studied in the last section and the present section must amount to a statement of Jesus' ontic divinity (i.e. his divine *being*, rather than merely divine *function*). The reason why John does not use the word 'God' of Jesus will be the same reason that accounts for the general slowness of this usage in becoming established Christian practice. He wants neither to say that Jesus simply is, without any distinction, the God Jesus called God and Father (a usage John reflects in 1:6; 2:28; 3:5, 12, 21), nor to seem to speak of two gods. But it is also notable that many times when he is talking most deliberately about God he does not call God 'God' either. He says far more about the deity of God by calling him 'the Alpha and the Omega' than he does by calling him 'God', and he also calls Jesus 'the Alpha and the Omega'.

WHAT CHRIST DOES, GOD DOES

The importance of John's extraordinarily high Christology for the message of Revelation is that it makes absolutely clear that what Christ does, God does. Since Christ shares the one eternal being of God, what Christ is said to do, in salvation and judgment, is no less truly and directly divine than what is said to be done by 'the One who sits on the throne'.

This is readily seen in relation to the parousia. In our last chapter, we have noticed that, in the designation of God as eternal in three tenses – 'the One who is and who was and who is to come' (1:4, 8; cf. 4:8) – the future of God is deliberately expressed by using the verb 'to come' (*ho erchomenos*), because God's future is conceived as his eschatological coming to the world in salvation and judgment. But this 'coming' of God to bring his purposes for his creation to fulfilment is the coming of Christ. For this future coming of Christ in glory, Revelation does not use the word *parousia*, which is common elsewhere in the New Testament, but it does regularly use the verb 'to come'. The hope and the warning of Christ's imminent coming dominate the book (1:7; 2:5, 16; 3:3, 11; 16:15; 22:7, 12, 20). Seven times in Revelation, Christ himself declares 'I am coming' (*erchomai*: 2:5, 16; 3:11; 16:15; 22:6, 12, 20).

His judgment at his coming is emphatically God's. For example, Revelation 22:12 follows common early Christian practice in quoting an Old Testament prophecy of God's coming to judgment (Isa. 40:10; 62:11) with reference to the parousia of Christ, and expands it with the well-known principle of divine judgment ('to repay according to everyone's work'), drawn here from Proverbs 24:12 (cf. Matt. 16:27; 1 Clem. 34:3; 2 Clem. 17:4). But if Christ's judgment at the parousia is the divine judgment, the same also must be said of his sacrificial death, which we shall see is also central to the theology of Revelation. When the slaughtered Lamb is seen 'in the midst of' the divine throne in heaven (5:6; cf. 7:17), the meaning is that Christ's sacrificial death *belongs to the way God rules the world*. The symbol of the Lamb is no less a divine symbol than the symbol of 'the One who sits on the throne'. In the last chapter we noticed the remoteness of 'the One who sits on the throne' in heaven from the world dominated by the powers of evil. While evil rules on earth, God as 'the One who sits on the throne' must be depicted only in heaven. Even the judgments, which issue from his holy presence in heaven and aim to bring about his rule on earth by destroying evil, derive from him only indirectly, through angelic intermediaries. But if God is not present in the world as 'the One who sits on the throne', he *is* present as the Lamb who conquers by suffering. Christ's suffering witness and sacrificial death are, in fact, as we shall see, the key event in God's conquest of evil and establishment of his kingdom on earth. Even more than the judgments which issue from the throne in heaven they constitute God's rule on earth. Moreover, Christ's presence (walking among the lampstands: 1:13; 2:1) with his people who continue his witness and sacrifice is also God's presence.

It follows that Revelation's Christology must be incorpo-

rated in our account of its understanding of God, supplement-
ing our previous chapter. God is related to the world not only
as the transcendent holy One, but also as the slaughtered
Lamb.

CHAPTER 4

The victory of the Lamb and his followers

STATISTICS

We saw in our chapter 2 that the sevenfold occurrence of divine designations in Revelation is John's way of highlighting their significance. It will be worth looking at the statistics of some christological designations, to prepare us for our study of the work of Christ in Revelation.

That the identification of Christ with God does not imply the unimportance of his humanity is indicated by the use of his particular human name Jesus. This occurs fourteen times in Revelation, seven of these in the phrases 'the witness of Jesus' (1:2, 9; 12:17; 19:10 (twice); 20:4) and 'the witnesses of Jesus' (17:6). As we shall see, what matters most about the humanity of Jesus in Revelation is the witness which he bore and which his followers continue.

The word 'Christ' (Messiah) occurs seven times (including occurrences of 'Jesus Christ'). As we shall see, Jesus' fulfilment of the Jewish hope of the Davidic Messiah is prominent in Revelation.

The word 'Lamb', referring to Christ, occurs 28 (7 × 4) times. Seven of these are in phrases coupling God and the Lamb together (5:13; 6:16; 7:10; 14:4; 21:22; 22:1, 3). Four is, after seven, the symbolic number most commonly and consistently used in Revelation. As seven is the number of completeness, four is the number of the world (with its four corners (7:1; 20:8) or four divisions (5:13; 14:7)). The first four judgments in each of the series of seven affect the world (6:8; 8:7–12; 16:2–9). The

7 × 4 occurences of 'Lamb' therefore indicate the worldwide scope of his complete victory. This corresponds to the fact that the phrase by which John designates all the nations of the world is *fourfold* ('peoples and tribes and languages and nations': the phrase varies each time it occurs, but is always fourfold) and occurs *seven* times (5:9; 7:9; 10:11; 11:9; 13:7; 14:6; 17:15). Its first occurrence establishes its connexion with the Lamb's victory (5:9).

THE MAJOR SYMBOLIC THEMES

The role of Christ in Revelation is to establish God's kingdom on earth: in the words of 11:15, to turn 'the kingdom of the world' (currently ruled by evil) into 'the kingdom of our Lord and his Messiah'. This is a work of both salvation and judgment. As we shall see, salvation and judgment are inevitably the two sides of a single coin. It is also a process which begins with his earthly life and death and ends with his parousia. The victory he has already achieved in his death and resurrection is decisive, but needs to be continued by his Christian followers in the present and completed at his parousia in the future. It will be important for us to distinguish these three stages, but also to understand the interconnexions between them. In order to find our way through the rather complex imagery in which John expresses his understanding of Christ's work, it will be helpful initially to recognize the three major symbolic themes – or complexes of symbols – which are all used of all three stages of the work of Christ. Each of the three enables us to see the essential unity of Christ's work, from cross to parousia. The combination of the three conveys most, if not all, of Revelation's distinctive theological interpretation of Christ's work.

The first is the theme of *the messianic war*. This takes up the Jewish hope for a Messiah who is to be a descendant of David, anointed by God as king and military leader of his people. He is to fight a war against the Gentile oppressors, liberating Israel and establishing the rule of God, which is also the rule of God's

Messiah and God's people Israel, over the nations of the world.[1] Essential to this notion, it should be noted, is that the Messiah does not wage war alone: he leads the army of Israel against the enemies of Israel. Many Old Testament prophecies were commonly interpreted by first-century Jews as referring to this expected Messiah of David. The identification of Jesus with the Davidic Messiah was, of course, very common in early Christianity. It is very important in Revelation, partly because for John, as a Jewish Christian prophet, it is one of the ways in which he can gather up the hopes of the Old Testament prophetic tradition into his own eschatological vision centred on Jesus. But it is important also because it portrays a figure who is to establish God's kingdom on earth by defeating the pagan powers who contest God's rule. As we shall see, John carefully reinterprets the tradition. His Messiah Jesus does not win his victory by military conquest, and those who share his victory and his rule are not national Israel, but the international people of God. But still it is a victory over evil, won not only in the spiritual but also in the political sphere against worldly powers in order to establish God's kingdom on earth. Insofar as the hope for the Davidic Messiah was for such a victory of God over evil Revelation portrays Christ's work in continuity with that traditional Jewish hope.

The prominence of Davidic messianism in Revelation can be gauged from the fact that, as well as the two self-declarations by Christ that we have already considered (1:17–18; 22:13), there is a third: 'I am the root and the descendant of David, the bright morning star' (22:16). The first of these two titles comes from Isaiah 11:10 ('the root of Jesse') and is used of the Davidic Messiah ('descendant' interprets the meaning of 'root', rightly giving it the same sense as the 'branch' or 'shoot' of Isa. 11:1, which was more commonly used as a messianic designation).

[1] For the messianic war, see E. Schürer, *The History of the Jewish People in the Age of Jesus Christ*, revised and ed. G. Vermes, F. Millar, M. Black, vol. II (Edinburgh: T. & T. Clark, 1979), 517–35; M. Hengel, *The Zealots* (Edinburgh: T. & T. Clark, 1989), 271–319; A. Yarbro Collins, 'The Political Perspective of the Revelation to John', *JBL* 96 (1977), 241–56; R. Bauckham, 'The Book of Revelation as a Christian War Scroll', *Neot.* 22 (1988), 17–40, which becomes chapter 8 in Bauckham, *The Climax of Prophecy*.

The second title refers to the star of Numbers 24:17, which (in the context of 24:17–19) was commonly understood to be a symbol of the Messiah of David who would conquer the enemies of Israel. 'The root of David' is found also in Revelation 5:1, alongside another title evoking the image of the royal Messiah who will defeat the nations by military violence: 'the Lion of Judah' (cf. Gen. 49:9; 4 Ezra 12:31–2). Further allusions to the Messiah of Isaiah 11, a favourite passage for Davidic messianism, are the sword that comes from Christ's mouth (1:16; 2:12, 16; 19:21) with which he strikes down the nations (19:15; cf. Isa. 11:4; 49:2) and the statement that he judges with righteousness (19:11; cf. Isa. 11:4).

One of John's key Old Testament texts, allusions to which run throughout Revelation, is Psalm 2, which depicts 'the nations' and 'the kings of the earth' conspiring to rebel against 'the LORD and his Messiah' (verses 1–2). The Messiah is God's Son (verse 7), whom he sets as king on mount Zion (verse 6), there to resist and overcome the rebellious nations. God promises to give this royal Messiah the nations for his inheritance (verse 8) and that he will violently subdue them with a rod of iron (verse 9). Allusions to this account of the Messiah's victory over the nations are found in Revelation 2:18, 26–8; 11:15, 18; 12:5, 10; 14:1; 16:14, 16; 19:15. To what is explicit in the psalm it is notable that John adds the Messiah's army (with him on Mount Zion in 14:1), who will share his victory (2:26–7). Probably also from the psalm is John's use of the phrase 'the kings of the earth' as his standard term for the political powers opposed to God which Christ will subdue (1:5; 6:15; 17:2, 18; 18:3, 9; 19:19; 21:24; cf. 16:14).

Also derived from this militant messianism is Revelation's key concept of conquering. It is applied both to the Messiah himself (3:21; 5:5; 17:14) and to his people, who share his victory (2:7, 11, 17, 28; 3:5, 12, 21; 12:11; 15:2; 21:7). Once again we note the importance in Revelation of the Messiah's army. That the image of conquering is a militaristic one should be unmistakable, although interpreters of Revelation do not always do justice to this. It is closely connected with language of battle (11:7; 12:7–8, 17; 13:7; 16:14; 17:14; 19:11, 19), and it is notable that not only do Christ's followers defeat the beast (15:2), but also the beast defeats them (11:7; 13:7), so that this is evidently a war in which Christ's enemies have their victories, though the final victory is his. We should note also that the language of conquering is used of all the three stages of Christ's work: he conquered in his death and resurrection (3:21; 5:5), his followers conquer in the time before the end (12:11; 15:2), and he will conquer at the parousia (17:14). Thus it is clear that the image of the messianic war describes the whole process of the establishment of God's kingdom as Revelation depicts it. Revelation's use of this image incorporates the fundamental shift of temporal perspective from Jewish to Jewish Christian eschatology. The messianic war is not purely future. The decisive victory has in fact already been won by Christ. His followers are called to continue the battle in the present. The final victory still lies in the future.

The second of the three major symbolic themes is that of *the eschatological exodus*. Since the exodus was the key salvation event of the history of Israel, in which God liberated his people from oppression in Egypt, destroyed their oppressors, made them his own people and led them to theocratic independence in a land of their own, it was naturally the model for prophetic and apocalyptic hopes of another great salvation event in the future. In some Jewish apocalyptic the eschatological intervention of God in which he will finally judge the evil powers and bring definitive salvation to his people was conceived as an eschatological exodus, surpassing the first exodus as eschatology surpasses history.[2] Traces of an interpretation of the saving work of Jesus Christ as bringing about the eschatological exodus can be found in many parts of the New Testament, but it is Revelation that develops the idea most fully.

The central image in this complex is that of Jesus himself as the Passover Lamb (first introduced at 5:6, 9–10). That Revelation's image of the Lamb refers to the lamb sacrificed at the Passover is clear especially from 5:9–10. There it is said that by his blood the Lamb has 'ransomed' a people and made them 'a

[2] Isa. 11:11–12:6; 43:14–21; 51:10–11; 1 Enoch 1:4; 1QM 1–2; Ap.Abr. 30:2–31:1; cf. Josephus, *Ant.* 20:97–8; Liv.Proph. 2:11–19; 12:12–13.

kingdom and priests serving our God'. The latter phrase echoes
the well-known words of the Sinai covenant (Exod. 19:5–6), by
which God made the people he had brought out of Egypt his
own people. God's liberation of his people from Egypt was
often referred to as his ransoming them from slavery to be his
own people (e.g. Deut. 7:8; 13:5), and the same image could be
used of the new exodus of the future (Isa. 35:10; 51:11). When
Revelation treats the blood of the Lamb as the price of redemption, this really goes beyond the role which the blood of the
Passover Lamb played in the exodus (cf. Exod. 12:12, 23).
Moreover, the Passover lamb played no role in Jewish expectation of a new exodus. But it is likely that in Revelation 5:6, 9
John alludes not only to the Passover lamb, but also to Isaiah
53:7, where the Suffering Servant is portrayed as a sacrificial
lamb.[3] He may well have connected this verse with the new
exodus language of Deutero-Isaiah and seen the Suffering
Servant of Isaiah 53 as the Passover lamb of the new exodus. In
any case, it is the central role which the death of Jesus played in
the Christian understanding of redemption which accounts for
the centrality of the Lamb to Revelation's use of the new
exodus motif.

In 15:2–4 the Christian martyrs, victorious in heaven, are
seen as the people of the new exodus, standing beside a
heavenly Red Sea, through which they have passed, and
singing a version of the song of praise to God which Moses and
the people of Israel sang after their deliverance from Pharaoh
at the Red Sea (Exod. 15). Moreover, the plagues which are
God's judgment on their enemies in this context (15:1,
5–16:21) are modelled on the plagues of Egypt at the time of
the exodus. We have already noticed, in chapter 2 above, that
the final judgment of this series is linked to a reminiscence of
the Sinai theophany (16:18). Other allusions to the exodus
narratives are in 11:6, where the activity of the two witnesses is
in part modelled on Moses and the plagues of Egypt, and 11:8,
where one of the prophetic names of the great city where the
witnesses are martyred is Egypt. Already in 2:14, the false

---

[3] Cf. allusions to Isa. 53 with reference to the passion of Christ elsewhere in the New
Testament, especially Luke 22:37; Heb. 9:28; 1 Pet. 2:22.

teachers in the church at Pergamum, who are persuading Christians to compromise with paganism, are compared with Balaam, the false prophet who was responsible for the seduction of the Israelites into idolatry, as a result of which they failed to reach the goal of the exodus: entry into the promised land.

As with the messianic war, John's use of the new exodus imagery shows that for him the decisive eschatological event has already occurred: the new Passover Lamb has been slaughtered and he has ransomed a people for God. The goal of the new exodus is still to be attained, when Christ's people will reign with him as priests on earth (20:4–6; 22:3–5), attaining their theocratic independence in the promised land. But Revelation's new exodus does not consistently follow the sequence of the Old Testament narrative. The imagery is used flexibly – in literal terms, inconsistently – to characterize all three stages of the work of Christ as Revelation portrays it.

The third theme which is used to characterize Christ's work is that of witness. Jesus himself is 'the faithful and true witness' (3:14; cf. 1:5). The title refers primarily to the witness which Jesus bore to God during his life on earth and to his faithfulness in maintaining his witness even at the cost of his life. The word 'witness' (*martys*) does not yet, in Revelation, carry the technical Christian meaning of 'martyr' (one who bears witness by dying for the faith). It does not refer to death itself as witness, but to verbal witness to the truth of God (cf. the association of witness with 'the word of God': 1:2, 9; 6:9; 20:4; cf. also 12:11) along with living obedience to the commands of God (cf. the association of witness with keeping the commandments: 12:17). But it is strongly implied that faithful witness will incur opposition and lead to death (2:13; 11:7; 12:17). That Jesus' witness led to his death is suggested by the sequence of titles in 1:5.

Jesus' work of witness is continued by his followers, who are not only called his witnesses (17:6; cf. 2:13) but are also said to hold 'the witness of Jesus' (12:17; 19:10), which is the same as their own witness (6:9; 12:11). 'The witness of Jesus' means not 'witness to Jesus', but the witness Jesus himself bore and which his faithful followers continue to bear. It is primarily Jesus' and his followers' witness to the true God and his righteousness, which exposes the falsehood of idolatry and the evil of those who worship the beast. The theme of witness is connected with Revelation's dominant concern with truth and falsehood. The world is a kind of court-room in which the issue of who is the true God is being decided. In this judicial contest Jesus and his followers bear witness to the truth. At the conclusion of the contest, their witness is seen to be true and becomes evidence on which judgment is passed against those who have refused to accept its truth: the beast and his worshippers. So, in the third stage of Christ's work, his parousia, the witness becomes the judge. He who was faithful and true as witness (3:14) is now called faithful and true in his activity of judgment (19:11).

If the title, 'the faithful witness' (1:5) for Christ is based on Psalm 89:37, there is a connexion with Davidic messianism, but John has certainly developed the theme of witness as a theme in its own right, as a judicial image alongside the military image of the messianic war which he also uses. His use of it may have been inspired by the prophecies of Deutero-Isaiah. These portray a judicial contest in which the claim of Yahweh to be the only true God, the Creator and the Lord of history, is vindicated against the gods of the nations. In this context the people of Israel are 'my witnesses' (Isa. 43:10, 12; 44:8), called to bear witness to all the nations that Yahweh alone is the true God and Saviour. The themes are close to those of Revelation, where, as we shall see, the emphasis is on the role of the church in bearing witness to all the nations (and against the idolatrous claims of the beast) that God is the only true God.

THE DEATH OF CHRIST

Fundamental to Revelation's whole understanding of the way in which Christ establishes God's kingdom on earth is the conviction that in his death and resurrection Christ has already won his decisive victory over evil. This conviction is portrayed in chapter 5, which is the continuation of the foundational vision of God's rule in heaven in chapter 4. After the revelation of God's sovereignty in heaven, which we studied in our chapter 2, the question of how his sovereignty is to become effective on earth is raised. John sees in the right hand of the One seated on the throne a sealed scroll (5:1). This contains the secret purpose of God for establishing his kingdom. Its contents are, in fact, what is to be revealed to John as the content of his prophecy for the churches. But it is established that only one person is qualified to open the scroll and divulge its contents. We shall have to identify the content of the scroll later. Here we are concerned with what it is that qualifies Jesus Christ to be the only one who can open it.

The key to John's vision of the slaughtered Lamb (5:6) is to recognize the contrast between what he hears (5:5) and what he sees (5:6). He hears that 'the Lion of the tribe of Judah, the Root of David, had conquered'. The two messianic titles evoke a strongly militaristic and nationalistic image of the Messiah of David as conqueror of the nations, destroying the enemies of God's people (cf., e.g., 1QSb 5:20–9). But this image is reinterpreted by what John sees: the Lamb whose sacrificial death (5:6) has redeemed people from all nations (5:9–10). By juxtaposing the two contrasting images, John has forged a new symbol of conquest by sacrificial death. The messianic hopes evoked in 5:5 are not repudiated: Jesus really is the expected Messiah of David (22:16). But insofar as the latter was associated with military violence and narrow nationalism, it is reinterpreted by the image of the Lamb. The Messiah has certainly won a victory, but he has done so by sacrifice and for the benefit of people from all nations (5:9). Thus the means by which the Davidic Messiah has won his victory is explained by the image of the Lamb, while the significance of the image of the Lamb is now seen to lie in the fact that his sacrificial death was a victory over evil.

Who or what it is that the Lamb has conquered is not expressed (cf. 3:21) (though it is probable that we should see the defeat of Satan by Michael, depicted in 12:7–9, as a symbol of the Lamb's victory). The object of conquest is left undefined in chapter 5 so that the victory should be boundless in its scope. All that is opposed to God's rule, we are to understand, has been defeated by the Lamb. Consequently, the acclamation of

the victorious Lamb expands, in anticipation of the eschatological fruits of his victory, to include the whole creation in the
worship of the One who sits on the throne together with the
Lamb (5:13). The continuing and ultimate victory of God over
evil which the rest of Revelation describes is no more than the
working-out of the decisive victory of the Lamb on the cross.

However, it is with the Lamb's victory as the basis for this
working-out that John is primarily concerned. He takes largely
for granted that Christ's sacrificial death has liberated Christians from sin (1:5) and made them the eschatological people of
God (1:5; 5:9–10). What is important, in the context of Revelation, about the church – as already constituted 'a kingdom and
priests serving our God' (5:10) – is the role it has to play in the
universal coming of the kingdom. The realization of God's rule
on earth already in the church cannot, in the universal perspective of Revelation, be the ultimate goal of Christ's victory. While
evil powers opposed to God dominate the earth, that victory has
still to reach its goal. But those who, as a result of it, already
acknowledge God's rule have, as we shall see, an indispensable
role to play in the full working-out of the Lamb's victory.

In chapter 5 the work of Christ already achieved is depicted in
the combination of the two motifs of messianic war and new
exodus. The third major motif, representing Christ as the faithful witness, is not explicitly related to these, so far as the depiction of the past work of Christ is concerned. But we can see the
relation of all three motifs in what is said about the way Christians share in Christ's victory over Satan:

> They have conquered him [Satan] by the blood of the Lamb
> and by the word of their testimony,
> for they did not cling to life even in the face of death.
>
> (12:11)

The whole verse requires that the reference to 'the blood of the
Lamb' is not purely to Christ's death but to the deaths of the
Christian martyrs, who, following Christ's example, bear
witness even at the cost of their lives.[4] But this witness even as far

---

[4] For this interpretation, cf. H. B. Swete, *The Apocalypse of St John* (London: Mac-
millan, second edn, 1907), 156; G. B. Caird, *The Revelation of St John the Divine*
(London: A. & C. Black, 1966), 156–7.

as death does not have an independent value of its own. Its value depends on its being a continuation of his witness. So it is by the Lamb's blood that they conquer. Their deaths defeat Satan only by participating in the victory the Lamb won over Satan by his death. This explanation of 12:11 has taken us already to the second stage of Christ's work – in which it is continued by his followers – but it shows that the element of faithful witness is essential to understanding how Christ's victory can take effect through the faithful discipleship of Christians in the world.

THE ARMY OF MARTYRS

When Christ's conquest is depicted and explained in 5:5–9, Revelation's readers and hearers already know that Christians are expected to conquer as Christ did. Each of the messages to the seven churches in chapters 2–3 had included a promise of eschatological reward to 'the one who conquers' (2:7, 11, 17, 26–8; 3:5, 12, 21), and the last of these, strategically placed in order to anticipate 5:5–6, reads: 'To the one who conquers, I will give a place with me on my throne, just as I myself conquered and sat down with my Father on his throne' (3:21). We first meet these victorious followers of Christ in chapter 7, which continues the theme of messianic war by depicting them as the army of the Davidic Messiah.[5]

Chapter 7:4–14 uses the same device as was used in 5:5–6: that of contrasting what John hears (7:4) and what he sees (7:9). The 144,000 from the twelve tribes of Israel (7:4–8) contrast with the innumerable multitude from all nations (7:9), but the two images depict the same reality. They are parallel to the two contrasting images of Christ in 5:5–6: the 144,000 Israelites are the followers of the Davidic Messiah, the Lion of Judah (note that the tribe of Judah is listed first), while the innumerable multitude are the people of the slaughtered Lamb, ransomed from all the nations (5:9). Just as the expectation of the Davidic Messiah was reinterpreted by means of the

---

[5] For the argument of this section in more detail, see Bauckham, 'The Book of Revelation as a Christian War Scroll' (n. 1 above).

scriptural image of the Passover lamb, so the purely nationalistic image of his followers is reinterpreted by an image drawn from the scriptural promises to the patriarchs. According to these, the descendants of the patriarchs would be innumerable (Gen. 13:16; 15:5; 32:12). Thus, not because Christians in the late first century were actually innumerable, but because of John's faith in the fulfilment of all the promises of God through Christ, the church is depicted as an innumerable company drawn from all nations.

However, there is a further contrast between the 144,000 Israelites and the innumerable multitude which makes the parallel with 5:5–6 exact. The 144,000 are an army. This is implicit in the fact that 7:4–8 is a census of the tribes of Israel. In the Old Testament a census was always a reckoning of the military strength of the nation, in which only males of military age were counted. The twelve equal contingents from the twelve tribes are the army of all Israel, reunited in the last days according to the traditional eschatological hope, mustered under the leadership of the Lion of Judah to defeat the Gentile oppressors of Israel. But the multitude who celebrate their victory in heaven, ascribing it to God and the Lamb (7:9–10), 'have washed their robes and made them white in the blood of the Lamb' (7:14). This means that they are martyrs, who have triumphed by participating, through their own deaths, in the sacrificial death of the Lamb. Admittedly, most commentators have understood 7:14 to refer to the Lamb's redemption of Christians from sin, but we have already seen that the reference to the blood of the Lamb in 12:11 must refer to martyrdom. Since 7:14 refers to an action of which the followers of the Lamb are subjects, it is parallel to 12:11, whereas in references to the redemption of Christians by Christ's blood, they are the objects of his action (1:5; 5:9).

Thus, just as 5:5–6 depicts Jesus Christ as the Messiah who has won a victory, but has done so by sacrificial death, not by military might, so 7:4–14 depicts his followers as the people of the Messiah who share in his victory, but do so similarly, by sacrificial death rather than by military violence. This interpretation is confirmed by 14:1–5, in which the 144,000 reappear. Chapters 12–14 portray the combatants in the messianic war. In chapters 12–13 the dragon, the beast and the second beast have been depicted successfully prosecuting war against the people of God (12:17; 13:7). But in 14:1 the Lamb and his army stand to oppose them on Mount Zion, the place of the messianic king's triumph over the hostile nations (Ps. 2:6). The much misunderstood reference to the virginity of the 144,000 (14:4a) belongs to the image of an army. The followers of Christ are symbolized as an army of adult males who, following the ancient requirement of ritual purity for those who fight in holy war (Deut. 23:9–14; 1 Sam. 21:5; 2 Sam. 11:9–13; 1QM 7:3–6), must avoid the cultic defilement incurred through sexual intercourse. This ritual purity belongs to the image of an army: its literal equivalent in John's ideal of the church is not sexual asceticism, but moral purity. But, just like the combination of the militaristic and sacrificial imagery for Christ in 5:5–6, so the image of an army changes to that of sacrifice in 14:4b–5, and with it the image of the ritual purity of the Lord's army changes to that of the perfection required in a sacrificial offering. The word which the NRSV translates 'blameless' (*amōmoi*) is cultic terminology for the physical perfection required in an animal acceptable for sacrifice (Exod. 29:38; Lev. 1:3; 3:1).

The cultic image is then translated into its literal equivalent: 'in their mouth no lie was found' (14:5). This relates to the theme of truth and falsehood, which is so important in Revelation, and evokes the third of the motifs which dominate Revelation's account of the work of Christ: that of faithful witness to the truth. But in using the words, 'in their mouth no lie was found', John is also echoing significant Old Testament texts: Zephaniah 3:13, which says of the eschatological people of God that 'a deceitful tongue shall not be found in their mouths', and Isaiah 53:9, which says of the Suffering Servant, who was 'led like a lamb to the slaughter' (53:7), that 'no lie was found in his mouth'. John exploits (in the manner of Jewish exegesis) the coincidence between these texts. The followers of the Lamb resemble the one they 'follow wherever he goes' (14:4). This following means imitating both his truthfulness, as 'the faithful witness', and the sacrificial death to which this led. Thus the victory of the Lamb's army is the victory of truthful witness maintained as far as sacrificial death. As in 12:11, the three images of messianic warfare, paschal sacrifice and faithful witness come together and mutually interpret one another.

To return to chapter 7, where the victory of the Lamb's followers through martyrdom is first depicted, it is important to notice its place in the structure of the visions. It intervenes between the sixth and seventh judgments of the first series of seven judgments: the seal-openings. The opening of the sixth seal seems to anticipate the immediate arrival of the final judgment (6:12–17), but this is delayed while the servants of God are sealed (7:1–3), an image which turns out to refer to their being marked out for martyrdom. We can now see how chapter 7 relates to the judgments of the seal-openings. When the fifth seal is opened, the Christian martyrs of the past cry out for their blood to be avenged, but they are told they must wait until the rest of the full complement of Christian martyrs is complete. In other words, the final judgment on the wicked, which will avenge the martyrs, is delayed until the rest of the Lamb's followers also suffer martyrdom. This is why their victory is depicted in an interlude between the sixth and seventh seal-openings. We may expect to find a further exposition of the same subject in the corresponding interlude in the next series of judgments: between the sixth and seventh trumpets.

What is the significance of martyrdom? In what sense is it a continuation of Christ's work by his followers, a working-out of the victory he achieved by his death? Reading only as far as chapter 7, it would seem that martyrdom is merely for the sake of the martyrs themselves. Taking the image of the new exodus in its most obvious sense, it seems that God's people, redeemed from all nations to be his own people (5:9), are delivered through martyrdom from the evil world. They triumph in heaven while their enemies on earth are doomed to final judgment. The judgment has been delayed only so that they can escape it through martyrdom. This is all that John's account up to and including chapter 7 can tell us. But thus far the real secret of God's purpose for the role of the church in the establishment of God's kingdom on earth has not been revealed to him. That occurs only in the interlude between the sixth and seventh judgments of the trumpet series (10:1–11:13).

THE UNSEALED SCROLL

We need to return to the scroll which the Lamb, because of his victory, is declared worthy to open (5:1–9).[6] The scroll is to reveal the way in which, according to the hitherto secret purpose of God, the Lamb's victory is to become effective in establishing God's rule over the world. Only the Lamb can open the scroll and reveal its contents, because it is his victory which makes possible the implementation of the purpose of God contained in the scroll. More specifically, as we shall see, the scroll will reveal how the followers of Christ are to participate in the coming of God's kingdom by following him in witness, sacrifice and victory. Because the Lamb has conquered, he is the one who can reveal how his followers are also to conquer.

The scroll is sealed with seven seals (5:1) and the Lamb opens the seals, one by one, from 6:1 to 8:1. But the events that occur at the opening of the seals are not, as interpreters of Revelation have too often supposed, the contents of the scroll. It would be a very odd scroll whose contents could be progressively revealed by the opening of a series of seals. The events of the seven seal-openings merely accompany the opening of the seals. The opening of the seals one by one is a literary device enabling John to narrate a series of visions which *prepare for* the revelation of the contents of the scroll. Neither the series of seven judgments which accompany the seal-openings, nor the series of seven trumpet-blasts which are closely attached to the opening of the seventh, final seal (cf. 8:1–6), is the content of the scroll.

The scroll itself, now opened, reappears in 10:2, 8–10. Most interpreters have been misled by the word used in 10:2, 9–10

---

[6] For the argument of this section and the next section in more detail, see chapter 9 ('The Conversion of the Nations') in Bauckham, *The Climax of Prophecy*.

(*biblaridion* is diminutive in form, but like many diminutive forms in the Greek of this period, need not differ in meaning from *biblion*, which is used in 5:1–9; 10:8) and have supposed the scroll of chapter 10 to be a different scroll from that of chapter 5. But John carefully indicates their identity.[7] The angel who brings the scroll down from heaven (10:1–2) is called 'another mighty angel' (10:1) in order to make a literary connection with 5:1–9, where the first 'mighty angel' is mentioned (5:2). More significantly, throughout chapters 4, 5 and 10, John is closely following the inaugural vision of the book of Ezekiel (Ezek. 1:1–3:11). Like Ezekiel, he sees a vision of the divine throne (Rev. 4; cf. Ezek. 1), which prepares for the communication of a prophetic message to the prophet. John's description of the scroll in the hand of God (5:1) is modelled on Ezekiel's similar description (Ezek. 2:9–10). In Ezekiel's case, God himself opens the scroll (2:10) and gives it to the prophet with the command to eat it (3:1–2). The eating of the scroll symbolizes the prophet's absorption of the divine message that he is to communicate. When Ezekiel eats it, it is sweet as honey in his mouth (Ezek. 3:3). In Revelation, the allusions to this Old Testament passage begin, as we have just indicated, in 5:1, and then continue in 10:2, 8–10, where an angel gives the open scroll to John and he eats it, finding it sweet as honey in his mouth, but bitter in his stomach. The difference between Ezekiel and Revelation lies in the opening of the scroll. In Revelation, the scroll must be opened by the Lamb before it can be given to John to eat. So the scroll is taken from the hand of God by the Lamb (5:7), who opens it (6:1, 3, 5, 7, 9, 12; 8:1). It is then taken from heaven to earth by an angel (10:1–2), who gives it to John to eat (10:8–10).

This chain of revelation, from God to the prophet John, corresponds exactly to 1:1, which states that the revelation which is the content of the book was given to God by Jesus Christ so that he might show it to his servants by sending his angel to his servant John (cf. also 22:16). We now understand

---

[7] This point is argued convincingly by F. D. Mazzaferri, *The Genre of the Book of Revelation from a Source-Critical Perspective* (Berlin and New York: de Gruyter, 1989), 265–79.

why the angel who is supposed to be a necessary link in this chain of revelation does not appear in the book until 10:1. It is not until chapter 10 that the main content of the prophetic revelation John communicates in his book is given to him. All that has preceded is preparatory – necessary to the understanding of this revelation, but not itself the revelation. Recognizing this is a vital, though neglected, key to understanding the book of Revelation.

The communication of the content of the scroll to John takes place as the first part of the extended interlude between the sixth and seventh trumpet blasts (10:1–11:13). It should be noted that the markers in 9:12 and 11:14 associate this interlude firmly with the sixth rather than the seventh trumpet. Why is the scroll given to John at this point, near the end of the second series of seven judgments? We noticed in chapter 2 above that all three series of judgments are closely related to the vision of God, as sovereign and holy, in Revelation 4. They bring God's holy will to bear on the evil world. But the judgments up to and including that of the sixth trumpet are strictly limited (see 6:8; 8:7–12; 9:5, 15, 18). They are warning judgments, designed to bring humanity to repentance. In 9:20–1, immediately before the interlude, it is clearly stated that they do not in fact have this effect. Those who survive the judgments do not repent. Judgments alone, it is implied, do not lead to repentance and faith.

This is why, early in the interlude, a further series of judgments – the seven thunders (10:3–4) – is apparently proposed only to be revoked. Unlike the scroll, they are to remain sealed and John is not to write their contents in his prophecy (10:4). In other words, the process of increasingly severe warning judgments is not to be extended any further. It is not that God's patience has run out, but that such judgments do not produce repentance. So the series of judgments affecting a quarter of the earth (6:8) and the series affecting a third of the earth (8:7–12; 9:15, 18) are not, as we might expect, followed by a series affecting half the earth. No doubt the seven thunders would have been such a series. But there is now to be only the final judgment, the seventh trumpet (10:7). When the content of the seventh trumpet is spelled out in detail as the seven bowls (15:1), they are total, not limited, judgments (16:2–21), accomplishing the final annihilation of the unrepentant.

If the seven thunders are not to occur and therefore remain sealed (10:4), what *is* revealed to John is the content of the scroll. This is God's hitherto unrevealed purpose for achieving what judgments alone have failed to achieve: the repentance of the world. Having eaten the scroll, John is told to reveal its contents by prophesying: 'You must prophesy again about many peoples and nations and languages and kings' (10:11). The word 'again' contrasts this prophecy not merely with John's activity as a prophet before now, but with all the previous prophetic revelation to which 10:7 refers. To prophets of both the Old and New Testament periods God had revealed his purpose of finally establishing his kingdom on earth, including all that John has hitherto described in his visions. What has not been revealed, except in hints which John now draws out, is the role of the followers of the Lamb in bringing the world to repentance and faith through their witness and death. It is a moot point whether the sentence just quoted from 10:11 should be translated, 'You must prophesy again *about* many peoples ...', or, 'You must prophesy again *to* many peoples ...' Either would make sense. John's prophecy is initially a revelation to the churches of the role they are to play as prophetic witnesses to the nations. But also, indirectly, it *is* the content of the prophetic witness of the churches to the nations.

The content of the scroll is revealed in summary immediately: in 11:1–13. This passage therefore contains, *in nuce*, the central message of John's whole prophecy. It is placed here to indicate how the church's witness to the nations intervenes before the final judgment, the seventh trumpet, with which God's kingdom finally comes (11:15–19). Then, in chapters 12–15, the church's victorious conflict with the powers of evil is given a much more extended treatment, which is then integrated into the extended account, which follows, of the final judgment and its results (15–22). The relation between 11:1–13 and chapters 12–15 can be seen from the way a series of new images are introduced in 11:1–13 with enigmatic brevity, anticipating their fuller treatment in the following chapters: the great city (11:8), the beast and his war against the saints (11:7), the symbolic time period (11:2–3) which is the period of the church's conflict with the beast. These images are taken up when the church's conflict with the beast is put in a larger context in chapters 12–15. But 11:1–13 itself gives John's fullest treatment of the way in which the church's witness secures the repentance and faith of the nations. So we must give it some close attention.

THE TWO WITNESSES

The content of the scroll is not that faithful Christians are to suffer martyrdom or that their martyrdom will be their victory: these things are already clear in 6:9–11; 7:9–14. The new revelation is that their faithful witness and death is to be instrumental in the conversion of the nations of the world. Their victory is not simply their own salvation from a world doomed to judgment, as might appear from chapter 7, but the salvation of the nations. God's kingdom is to come not simply by saving an elect people who acknowledge his rule from a rebellious world over which his kingdom prevails merely by extinguishing the rebels. It is to come as the sacrificial witness of the elect people who already acknowledge God's rule brings the rebellious nations also to acknowledge his rule. The people of God have been redeemed *from all the nations* (5:9) in order to bear prophetic witness *to all the nations* (11:3–13).

This is what the story of the two witnesses (11:3–13) symbolically dramatizes. Two individuals here represent the church in its faithful witness to the world. Their story must be taken neither literally nor even as an allegory, as though the sequence of events in this story were supposed to correspond to a sequence of events in the church's history. The story is more like a parable, which dramatizes the nature and the result of the church's witness. Thus we should not, for example, suppose the story to imply that only after all faithful Christians have completed their witness and suffered martyrdom will they be vindicated in the eyes of their enemies and the latter be converted. The story is more likely to dramatize what will be happening all the time while Christians bear faithful witness to the world.

That the two witnesses symbolize the church in its role of witnessing to the world is shown by the identification of them as lampstands (11:4), the symbol of the churches in chapter 1, where the seven churches are represented as seven lampstands (1:12, 20). That they are only two does not indicate that they are only part of the whole church, but corresponds to the well-known biblical requirement that evidence be acceptable only on the testimony of two witnesses (Deut. 19:15). They are therefore the church insofar as it fulfils its role as faithful witness. As witnesses they are also prophets (11:3, 10), modelled especially on the Old Testament figures of Elijah and Moses (11:5–6; cf. 2 Kings 1:10–12; 1 Kings 17:1; Exod. 7:14–24).[8] But they are not Elijah and Moses *redivivi*, since the powers of both Elijah and Moses are attributed to both witnesses (11:6). Nor do Moses and Elijah here stand for the law and the prophets. Both are prophets. As prophets who both confronted the world of pagan idolatry they set the precedent for the church's prophetic witness to the world.

Moses and Elijah did not suffer martyrdom, but in New Testament times this was often thought to have been the fate of most of the Old Testament prophets and virtually the expected fate of any prophet. However, 11:8 shows that the principal precedent for the death of the two witnesses is that of Jesus. The parallel continues with their resurrection and ascension after three and a half days (11:11–12): John has converted the three days of the Gospel story into the conventional apocalyptic number three and a half. So it is the witness of Jesus himself that the witnesses continue, and their death is a participation in the blood of the Lamb. It is also clear from the universalistic language of 11:9–10 that it is a witness to all nations. The city

---

[8] This distinguishes Rev. 11 from the widespread apocalyptic tradition about the return of Enoch and Elijah. The forms of this tradition which are closest to Rev. 11 (in expecting the martyrdom of the two prophets) have been influenced by Rev. 11: see R. Bauckham, 'The Martyrdom of Enoch and Elijah: Jewish or Christian?', *JBL* 95 (1976), 447–58.

which is the scene of their prophecy, death and vindication cannot be Jerusalem, in spite of the reference to Jesus' crucifixion there (11:8), but because of that reference nor can it be only Rome, to which, under the symbol of Babylon, 'the great city' refers elsewhere in Revelation (14:8; 18:16, 18, 19, 21). It is any and every city in which the church bears its prophetic witness to the nations.

Judgments alone do not lead to repentance (9:20–1). The witness of the witnesses does lead to repentance, though not independently of judgments, but in conjunction with them (11:6, 13). The point is not simply that their witness to the true God and his righteousness reinforces the evidence of judgments, though it is certainly the case that their perseverance in witness even at the cost of their lives is powerful evidence. Nor is it even simply that the judgments are only intelligible as the judgments of God when accompanied by verbal witness. The point is rather that judgments themselves do not convey God's gracious willingness to forgive those who repent. Although the general impression of the witnesses the passage gives might seem to be severe, we should give full weight, since it is the one indication of what they say, to the fact that they are dressed in sackcloth (11:3), the symbol of repentance (cf. Jonah 3:4–10; Matt. 11:21; Luke 10:13). This means that, confronted with a world addicted to idolatry and evil (9:20–1), they proclaim the one true God and his coming judgment on evil (cf. 14:7), but they do so *as a call to repentance*. Therefore, once their witness is seen, not to be refuted by their death, but vindicated as the truth (11:11–13), all who see this repent. Verse 13 certainly means that all the survivors genuinely repent and acknowledge the one true God. The description of their response corresponds to the invitation of the angel who, in 14:6–7, calls on all nations to acknowledge God. It also contrasts with 9:20–1 (cf. 16:9–11). After the judgments of the trumpets, 'the rest' (*hoi loipoi*) did not repent (9:20); after the earthquake which accompanied the vindication of the witnesses, 'the rest' (*hoi loipoi*) feared God and gave him glory (11:13).

The remarkably universal, positive result of the witnesses'

testimony is underlined by the symbolic arithmetic of 11:13. In the judgments announced by Old Testament prophets a tenth part (Isa. 6:13; Amos 5:3) or seven thousand people (1 Kings 19:18) are the faithful remnant who are spared when the judgment wipes out the majority. In a characteristically subtle use of allusion, John reverses this. Only a tenth suffers the judgment, and the 'remnant' (*hoi loipoi*) who are spared are the nine-tenths. Not the faithful minority, but the faithless majority are spared, so that they may come to repentance and faith. Thanks to the witness of the witnesses, the judgment is actually salvific. In this way, John indicates the novelty of the witness of the two witnesses over against the Old Testament prophets whom he has used as their precedents. This is especially the case in that the reference to the seven thousand alludes to the effect of Elijah's ministry. Elijah was to bring about the judgment of all except the faithful seven thousand, who were spared (1 Kings 19:14–18). The two witnesses will bring about the conversion of all except the seven thousand, who are judged. Of course, the contrast is made in symbolic terms, and so it would be inappropriate to wonder why the seven thousand could not also have been converted.

To be the witnesses who bring the nations to faith in the one true God is the novel role of God's eschatological people, revealed by the scroll that only the Lamb has been able to open. If we ask how the prophetic witness of the church is able to have this effect, which that of the Old Testament prophets did not, the answer is no doubt that it derives its power from the victory of the Lamb himself. His witness had the power of a witness maintained even to the point of death and then vindicated as true witness by his resurrection. The witness of his followers participates in this power when they too are faithful witnesses even to death. The symbolic narrative of 11:11–12 means not that the nations have to see the literal resurrection of the Christian martyrs before they are convinced of the truth of their witness, but that they have to perceive the martyrs' participation in Christ's triumph over death. In fact, the way that Christian martyrdom, in the early centuries of the church, impressed and won people to faith in the Christian God, was precisely thus. The martyrs were effective witnesses to the truth of the Gospel because their faith in Christ's victory over death was so convincingly evident in the way they faced death and died.

DEFEATING THE BEAST

Of the three major symbolic motifs we have been tracing – the messianic war, the new exodus and witness – it is, of course, the third that dominates the story of the two witnesses (11:3–13), although there are hints of the messianic war (11:7) and the new exodus (11:6, 8). These hints are taken up and developed in chapters 12–15, which treat at greater length the same theme of the role of the faithful followers of Christ in the coming of God's kingdom. In this section we shall consider the theme of messianic war in chapters 12–14.[9]

The call to Revelation's readers or hearers to 'conquer' is fundamental to the structure and theme of the book. It demands the readers' active participation in the divine war against evil. Everything else that is said in the seven messages to the churches has this aim, expressed in the promise to the conquerors that concludes each (2:7, 11, 17, 28; 3:5, 12, 21): to enable the readers to take part in the struggle to establish God's universal kingdom against all opposition. The eschatological content of the promises, as well as the single promise to the conquerors which matches them at the climax of the whole book in 21:7, shows that it is only by conquering that the members of the churches may enter the New Jerusalem (cf. 22:14). The visions that intervene between the seven messages to the churches and the final vision of the New Jerusalem are to enable the readers to move from one to the other, to understand what conquering involves.

The verb 'to conquer' is left intriguingly without an object (except once, when the beast is its subject: 11:7) until chapter 12. This is because it is only in chapters 12–13 that the principal enemies of God, who must be defeated to make way

---

[9] For the argument of this section in more detail, see Bauckham, 'The Book of Revelation as a Christian War Scroll' (n. 1 above).

for his kingdom, are introduced. They are the satanic trinity: the dragon or serpent (the primeval, supernatural source of all opposition to God), the beast or sea-monster (the imperial power of Rome), and the second beast or earth-monster (the propaganda machine of the imperial cult).[10] (Babylon, the great harlot, who represents the corrupt and exploitative civilization of the city of Rome, supported by the political and military power of the empire, is not properly introduced until chapter 17, but she has a rather different status. Christians are not called to conquer her, but to 'come out of her' (18:4), i.e. to dissociate themselves from her evil.) The powerful mythic resonances of the images of chapters 12–13 place the coming confrontation between Christians and the power of Rome in the perspective of the cosmic war of evil against God and his faithful people. The initial confrontation between the serpent and the woman who bears the child who will defeat him in the end (12:1–5) takes the story back to the garden of Eden (cf. Gen. 3:15), and, since the woman is not only Eve but also Zion, from whom the Messiah is born (cf. Isa. 66:7–9), also takes in the history of pre-Christian Israel. Some of the oldest mythological images of the divine Warrior's victory over the monsters of chaos are revived. The dragon is Leviathan, the seven-headed serpent whom the Lord with his great sword will punish on the last day (Isa. 27:1), while the ancestry of the beast also goes back (via the monsters of Daniel 7:2–8) to Leviathan, since he rises out of the sea. Moreover, the conjunction of the sea-monster and the earth-monster (13:1, 11) echoes the traditional pair of monsters, Leviathan and Behemoth, rulers respectively of sea and land. Thus the bestial figures are

[10] For these three figures, their mythical background and their historical reference in Revelation, see G. R. Beasley-Murray, *The Book of Revelation* (London: Marshall, Morgan & Scott, 1974), 191–221; A. Yarbro Collins, *The Combat Myth in the Book of Revelation* (Harvard Dissertations in Religion 9; Missoula, Montana: Scholars Press, 1976), chapter 4; J. M. Court, *Myth and History in the Book of Revelation* (London: SPCK, 1979), chapter 6; F. R. McCurley, *Ancient Myths and Biblical Faith* (Philadelphia: Fortress Press, 1983), chapters 2–3; S. R. F. Price, *Rituals and Power: The Roman Imperial Cult in Asia Minor* (Cambridge University Press, 1984), 62–4; R. Bauckham, 'The *Figurae* of John of Patmos', in Ann Williams, ed., *Prophecy and Millenarianism: Essays in Honour of Marjorie Reeves* (London: Longman, 1980), 107–25: revised version (chapter 6: 'The Lion, the Lamb and the Dragon') in Bauckham, *The Climax of Prophecy*.

essentially primeval forces of evil, destined for ultimate defeat by the divine Warrior at the last day, but currently incarnated in the oppressive power of the Roman Empire, which surpasses in its military violence and its deification of its own power even the evil empires of the past (Dan. 7:2–8).

It is these intimidating forces that Christians, as the Lamb's army (14:1–5), are called on to defeat by their faithful witness to the point of death, that is, by the blood of the Lamb. They have already so defeated the dragon (12:11). Now that, cast down from heaven, he musters his forces on earth in the form of the imperial power (12:12, 18–13:2), they must defeat the beast (15:2). But the use of the verb 'to conquer' is not so simple. It is also said, as already anticipated in 11:7, that the beast 'was allowed to make war on the saints and to conquer them' (13:12). The point is not that the beast and the Christians each win some victories; rather, the same event – the martyrdom of Christians – is described both as the beast's victory over them and as their victory over the beast. In this way John poses the question: who are the real victors? The answer depends on whether one sees things from the earthly perspective of those who worship the beast or from the heavenly perspective which John's visions open up for his readers. To the inhabitants of the earth (13:8) it is obvious that the beast has defeated the martyrs. The political and military might of the beast, which seems to carry all before it and wins the admiration and the worship of the world, here seems triumphant even over the witnesses of Jesus. That it can put the Christian martyrs to death apparently with impunity seems the final proof of the invincible, godlike might of the beast. In the judicial contest as to who is the true God – the beast or the one to whom the martyrs witness – it seems the verdict is clear: the evidence of the martyrs has been refuted.

Even Christians must have been tempted to see it that way. They were a tiny minority of powerless people up against the overwhelming might of the state and the overwhelming pressure of pagan society. To refuse to compromise was to become even more helpless victims. What was the point of resisting the beast when he was proving irresistible? But John's message is that from the heavenly perspective things look quite different. The martyrs are the real victors. To be faithful in witness to the true God even to the point of death is not to become a victim of the beast, but to take the field against him and win. But only in a vision of heaven (7:9–14; 15:2–3) or a voice from heaven (11:12; 14:2) can the martyrs be *recognized* as victors. The perspective of heaven must break into the earthbound delusion of the beast's propaganda to enable a different assessment of the same empirical fact: the beast's apparent victory is the martyrs' – and therefore God's – real victory.

The heavenly perspective has the power of truth. When the martyrs testify to the true God against the spurious divine claims of the beast and refuse to admit the lies of the beast even when they could evade death by doing so, they win the victory of truth over deceit. The beast's lies cannot deceive them or even win their lip-service by coercion. He can kill them, but he cannot suppress their witness to the truth. Their death does not refute their evidence, because even in their death the power of truth to convince overcomes the power of mere physical might to suppress it. Hence perhaps the most important contrast between the forces of evil and the army of the Lamb is the contrast between deceit and truth. The dragon is the one who deceives the whole world (12:9; cf. 20:2–3, 7–8), the second beast deceives the inhabitants of the earth with its propaganda for the divinity of the beast (13:14; cf. 19:21), Babylon deceives all nations with her sorceries (18:23), but the followers of the Lamb, like the Lamb himself, are entirely without deceit (14:5; cf. 3:14).

So the theme of messianic war has brought us back to the theme of witness to the truth. As usual, John's major themes serve to interpret one another. But the theme of the messianic war has its own importance. By using the military image for both assessments of what is happening when the martyrs die – the beast is victorious, the Lamb is victorious – John is able to pose most effectively the crucial issue of how one sees things. Is the world a place in which military and political might carries all before it or is it one in which suffering witness to the truth prevails in the end? Thus Revelation offers its readers prophetic discernment guided by the core of Christian faith: that Jesus Christ won his comprehensive victory over all evil by suffering witness. It also calls for courageous adherence to that discernment in practice, as the calls 'for the endurance and faithfulness of the saints' (13:10; cf. 14:12), inserted into the portrayal of the messianic war, indicate. Whereas modern terminology calls martyrdom 'passive resistance', John's military imagery makes it just as active as any physical warfare. While rejecting the apocalyptic militancy that called for literal holy war against Rome, John's message is not, 'Do not resist!' It is, 'Resist! – but by witness and martyrdom, not by violence.' On the streets of the cities of Asia, John's readers are not to compromise but to resist the idolatry of the pagan state and pagan society. In so doing they will be playing an indispensable part in the working-out of the Lamb's victory.

Does John expect that, in the impending conflict with the power of the Roman Empire, all faithful Christians will suffer martyrdom? He certainly writes as though he did. Although in Revelation the term 'to conquer' does not simply mean to die as a martyr, it certainly includes death (12:11). Christians conquer the beast by their faithful witness to the truth of God up to and including death for maintaining this witness. In this way their faithful witness to the point of death participates in the power of the victory Christ won by his faithful witness to the point of death: they conquer 'by the blood of the Lamb' (12:11; cf. 7:14). But 'conquering' is not represented in Revelation as something to which only some Christians are called. The promises to the conquerors at the end of each of the seven messages to the churches present conquering as the only way for Christians to reach their eschatological destiny. The point is reinforced by the promise God himself gives the conquerors in 21:7, where there are clearly only two options: to conquer and inherit the eschatological promises, or to suffer the second death in the lake of fire (21:8). The same alternatives are presented as the only choices for John's readers in 22:14–15 (where those 'who wash their robes' (i.e. in the blood of the Lamb) are the martyrs: cf. 7:14).

Many interpreters have been understandably reluctant to

accept that John envisages the martyrdom of all Christians without exception, but it is what these passages clearly imply. On the other hand, John seems to be quite capable of also writing as though there will be faithful Christians still alive at the parousia (3:20; 16:15). This suggests that, on this issue as on many others, Revelation has suffered from interpretation which takes its images too literally. Even the most sophisticated interpreters all too easily slip into treating the images as codes which need only to be decoded to yield literal predictions. But this fails to take the images seriously as images. John depicts the future in images in order to be able to do both more and less than a literal prediction could. Less, because Revelation does not offer a literal outline of the course of future events – as though prophecy were merely history written in advance. But more, because what it does provide is insight into the nature of God's purpose for the future, and does so in a way that shapes the readers' attitudes to the future and invites their active participation in the divine purpose.

In this light, we can see why Revelation portrays the future *as though* all faithful Christians will be martyred. The message of the book is that if Christians are faithful to their calling to bear witness to the truth against the claims of the beast, they will provoke a conflict with the beast so critical as to be a struggle to the death. The imagery of chapters 13–14 absolutizes this situation in order to reveal what is really at stake. The beast will tolerate no dissent from his self-deification. Witness to the truth is inconsistent with any compromise with his lies. Therefore the alternative becomes the utterly stark one: worship the beast or face martyrdom. The portrayal of the situation such that no one can escape this choice in this stark form embodies John's prophetic insight into the issue between the church and the empire: that there can be no compromise between the truth of God and the idolatrous lie of the beast. It is an insight characteristic of the biblical prophetic tradition (cf. 1 Kings 18:21). It is not a literal prediction that every faithful Christian will in fact be put to death. But it does require that every faithful Christian must be prepared to die. The call to conquer allows no middle ground where Christians may hope to avoid death by compromising with the beast. In the situation John envisages, martyrdom belongs, as it were, to the essential nature of faithful witness. Not every faithful witness will actually be put to death, but all faithful witness requires the endurance and the faithfulness (13:10) that will accept martyrdom if it comes. If we must translate the call to conquer into literal terms, we could say that it requires every Christian already to accept the martyrdom that faithful witness may incur.

THE HARVEST OF THE EARTH[11]

Chapters 12–14 depict the messianic war from the incarnation (12:5) to the parousia (14:14–20). But the militaristic imagery is abandoned before the end of the account in favour of other images. In chapter 13 we see the beast waging war on the saints. In 14:1–5 we see the martyrs, the Lamb's army, success-fully resisting attack on mount Zion and celebrating their triumph in heaven. But even before the end of the description of these followers of the Lamb, the imagery has shifted from military terms to those of sacrifice and witness (14:4b–5). The effect of the martyrs' victory on the nations (14:6–11) and the final outcome of the war at the parousia (14:14–20) are then depicted in images quite different from those of messianic war. The reason is, as we already know from 11:3–13, that the purpose of the participation of the Lamb's followers in the messianic war is to bring the nations to repentance and faith in the true God. This cannot be depicted in the imagery of war.

Therefore the effect of the martyrs' witness on the nations is depicted in the three angelic proclamations of 14:6–11, addressed to the same universal constituency as submit to the beast's rule and worship him (14:6; cf. 13:7–8). The conflict between the beast and the Christian martyrs confronts the nations with the choice: heed the witness of the martyrs and repent of idolatry (14:7) or face the judgment of God on all who worship the beast (14:9–11). The result of this choice, the

---

[11] For the argument of this section and the next section in more detail, see chapter 9 ('The Conversion of the Nations') in Bauckham, *The Climax of Prophecy*.

outcome of the whole conflict, is then depicted in a new image – a traditional image of the eschatological consummation, but introduced only at this point in Revelation. This is the image of the harvest, which John presents in two forms: the grain harvest (14:14–16) and the vintage (14:17–20). The double image comes from Joel 3:13. Although this verse actually depicts the two stages of the grape harvest, the Hebrew word used for harvest is most commonly used for the grain harvest and so John has read it in that sense (and he was not the first to do so: cf. Mark 4:29). In this way he has drawn from Joel two images – the grain harvest and the vintage – both of which were in any case well-established images of the eschatological consummation (e.g. Isa. 63:1–4; Matt. 13:39–42; Mark 4:29; 4 Ezra 4:28-32; 2 Bar. 70:2). He has used the two images to depict the two aspects, positive and negative, of the parousia: the gathering of the converted nations into Christ's kingdom and the final judgment of the unrepentant nations. This interpretation of the two images has only rarely been accepted by previous interpreters of Revelation, but John has clearly indicated it in three ways.

In the first place, each of the two images is connected to an image earlier in the chapter. The 'great winepress of the wrath of God' (14:19) echoes both 'the wine of the wrath of her fornication' (14:8), which Babylon has made all nations drink, and 'the cup of the wine of the anger of God poured undiluted into the cup of his wrath' (14:10),[12] which God makes all who have worshipped the beast drink. Babylon's wine is the corrupting way of life which she offered the nations and thereby enticed them to worship the beast. God's wine is the judgment on the nations (as can also be seen from the allusion to Isaiah 63:3, which is here combined with Joel 3:13).

The corresponding antecedent to the image of the grain harvest is in 14:4: the 144,000 'have been ransomed from humanity as first fruits for God and the Lamb'. The phrase recalls 5:9, addressed to the Lamb: 'by your blood you ransomed for God [people] from every tribe and language and

---

[12] *thymos*, translated 'wrath' in both these phrases, may mean 'passion' in the first (cf. also 18:3), but is clearly meant to link the two phrases.

people and nation'. But now we learn that the followers of the
Lamb, ransomed by his sacrifice, are to be themselves a sacrifice. Moreover, they are a specific kind of sacrifice: first fruits.
The first fruits were the first sheaf which was taken from the
harvest before the rest was reaped, and which was then offered
to God as a sacrifice (Lev. 23:9–14). The connexion between
the first fruits of 14:4 and the reaping of the whole harvest in
14:14–16 would be obvious to any Jew, who was unlikely to be
able to use the image of the first fruits without implying a full
harvest of which the first fruits are the token and pledge
(cf. Rom. 8:23; 11:16; 16:5; 1 Cor. 15:20, 23; 16:15). Thus the
martyrs, redeemed *from* all the nations, are offered to God as
the first fruits of the harvest *of* all the nations, whose reaping is
depicted in 14:14–16.

Secondly, although the descriptions of the harvest and the
vintage are in many respects parallel, there is a major difference between them. The grain harvest takes place in only one
action: reaping. The vintage comprises two actions: gathering
the grapes into the winepress and treading the winepress.
These two actions, we learn later in Revelation, correspond to
the gathering of the kings of the earth and their armies to
Armageddon (16:12–14) and the judgment of the nations at
the parousia (19:15, which echoes 14:19 and reveals the
identity of the one who treads the winepress, left enigmatic in
14:20). The account of the grain harvest could have been
extended in parallel to the vintage, for reaping was followed by
threshing (usually performed by animals trampling the grain)
and winnowing (in which the good grain was separated from
the chaff, which blew away or was burned). Just as treading
the winepress is a natural image of judgment, so are threshing
and winnowing. But reaping is not. When the harvest is used as
an image of judgment, either threshing is the aspect specified
(Jer. 51:33; Mic. 4:12–13; Hab. 3:12; Matt. 3:12; Luke 3:17;
cf. Rev. 11:2) or the wicked are compared with the chaff blown
away by the wind or burned (Ps. 1:4; 35:5; Isa. 17:13; 29:5;
Dan. 2:35; Hos. 13:3; Matt. 3:12; Luke 3:17). Discriminatory
judgment could be symbolized by the gathering of the grain
into the barns, while the weeds (removed before reaping) or

the chaff are burned (Matt. 3:12; 13:30; Luke 3:17). Hardly ever is harvest, as such, a negative image of judgment (Hos. 6:11), while the specific action of reaping never is. With reference to the eschatological consummation, reaping is always a positive image of bringing people into the kingdom (Mark 4:29; John 4:35–8). Modern urban readers, not used to thinking about unmechanized agricultural processes, do not naturally bother to discriminate among biblical harvest images. But ancient readers differed from us in this respect. The actions depicted were very familiar to them. They would immediately notice that Revelation's picture of the grain harvest does not proceed to the processes which symbolized judgment, while that of the vintage does.

Thirdly, the single action in the grain harvest is performed by 'one like a son of man', seated on a cloud and wearing a crown (14:14), whereas the two actions of the vintage are performed respectively by an angel (14:19) and one whose identity is not revealed until 19:11–16 depicts him as the divine warrior and judge. The figure who reaps the grain harvest is certainly Jesus Christ (cf. 1:13) and so is the one who treads the winepress, but the two images of Christ are different. The description of the figure on the cloud is a precise allusion to Daniel 7:13–14, the only verses in Daniel which refer to 'one like a son of man'. They depict him coming on clouds to God (compare the relation of the cloud to the heavenly temple in Revelation 14:14–15) to receive dominion over 'all peoples, nations and languages' (7:14; compare the golden crown which the figure in Revelation 14:14 wears). Daniel 7 does not depict this figure as a judge or as concerned in the destruction of the beast. He simply receives his universal kingdom. This is also what he does in Revelation 14:14–16. He receives into his kingdom the nations which have been won from the beast's dominion for Christ's by the martyrs' conquest of the beast. Unlike the Gospel traditions in which Jesus is called 'the Son of man', John carefully uses the exact phrase from Daniel, 'one like a son of man', and uses it only here and in 1:13. He does not associate Daniel 7:13–14 with Christ's parousia as judge, as some early Christian writers do, but restricts the christological reference of the passage to what it actually says, which closely related to his own interest in Christ's rule over all the nations. In 1:13 Christ is depicted as the one who has authority already over the churches, but as we now know he constituted the churches a kingdom for God only so that they, by their witness in the world, could participate in bringing all the nations into the kingdom of God and his Christ (11:15). He is 'one like a son of man' precisely in relation to the churches *as lampstands* (1:12–13), bearing light for the nations. In 14:14–16 we see Christ's kingdom extended from the church to the nations.

So in 14:14–20 John depicts the outcome of history in two contrasting images – the positive 'harvest of the earth' and the negative 'vintage of the earth'. This is rather different from 11:13, where the story of the church's witness ends with the conversion of all who survive the warning judgments. The difference corresponds to the fact that in chapters 13–14 the power and deception of the beast have been presented and the ambiguity of the conflict between the beast and the martyrs highlighted. It is an open question whether the nations will accept the witness of the martyrs and perceive their death as victory over the beast or whether they will persist in delusion and continue to worship the beast who appears to triumph over the martyrs. The double conclusion to chapter 14 corresponds to the two possibilities opened by the proclamation of the angels (14:6–11). We shall return to this issue after considering the third and final passage in which Revelation depicts the effect of the witness of the martyrs in converting the nations (15:2–4).

THE CONVERSION OF THE NATIONS

In this passage it is the new exodus motif which is used to depict the effect of the church's witness to the nations. In 15:2 the martyrs are seen to have come triumphantly out of their conflict with the beast. Their passage through martyrdom to heaven is compared with the passage of the Israelites through the Red Sea, for the sea of glass in heaven (cf. 4:6) is now mingled with the fire of divine judgment (15:2). They stand beside the sea, praising God for the victory he has wrought for them, just as the people of Israel, led by Moses, sang a song of praise to God for his deliverance of them from Pharaoh's army (Exod. 15:1–18). Because the new exodus is the victory the martyrs have won, by the blood of the Lamb (cf. 7:14; 12:11), their song is not only the song of Moses but also the song of the Lamb.

The words of the martyrs' song are not, however, those of the song of Moses in Exodus 15:1–18; but nor are they simply another song, with which John has replaced the original song of Moses. Like the version of the song of Moses which Isaiah 12 predicts that Israel will sing at the new exodus, Revelation's version is an *interpretation* of the song of Moses, which John has produced by typically skilful use of current Jewish exegetical methods. As he related the hymn of Exodus 15 to the eschatological exodus, John evidently identified five points of significance:

(1) God's mighty act of judgment on his enemies, which was also the deliverance of his people. (Exod. 15:1–10, 12)
(2) God's mighty act of judgment demonstrated God's incomparable superiority to the pagan gods:
> Who is like you, O LORD, among the gods?
> Who is like you, majestic in holiness,
> awesome in splendour, doing wonders?
>
> (Exod. 15:11)
(3) God's mighty act of judgment filled the pagan nations with fear. (Exod. 15:14–16)
(4) It brought his people into his temple. (Exod. 15:13, 17)
(5) The song concludes: 'The Lord shall reign forever and ever'. (Exod. 15:18)

The words with which the song ends (5) clearly connect with Revelation's overall theme of the establishment of God's eschatological kingdom, and so John has already quoted them at 11:15. The significance of the new exodus for him is ultimately that it leads to God's eternal kingdom. Point (1) is reflected in the references to God's deeds, ways and judgments (Rev. 15:3–4), and point (4) is fulfilled in the presence of the martyrs in the heavenly sanctuary (15:2: implied by the sea of glass, which is before the divine throne, according to 4:6). But it is notable that the deliverance of God's people, though presupposed, is not mentioned in Revelation's version of the song. Point (2) is plainly relevant to Revelation's concern with demonstrating the incomparability of the one true God against the idolatrous pretensions of the beast. Therefore the words with which the whole world worships the beast in 13:4 are in fact a parody of these words from the song of Moses: 'Who is like the beast, and who can fight against it?' John understands the new exodus as God's demonstration of his incomparable deity to the nations, refuting the beast's claim to deity. Therefore also point (4) falls into place: God demonstrates his deity so that the nations 'fear God and give him glory' (14:7). This has become in fact the main point of the interpretation of the song given by the version in Revelation 15:3–4. In Exodus 15, God's mighty act of judgment and deliverance inspires terror in the pagan nations. This is indeed, in the context, a recognition of his incomparable deity, but its significance remains rather negative. John has reinterpreted it in a strongly positive sense, as referring to the repentance of all the nations and their acknowledgment and worship of the one true God.

He has arrived at this interpretation of the song of Moses by way of two other Old Testament passages, which he has used to interpret it and both of which he quotes in his own version of the song. He has connected these passages with the song of Moses because both have parallels to the song's key verse (Exod. 15:11) about the incomparability of God. In the following quotations, the words parallel to Exodus 15:11 are underlined, those quoted in Revelation 15:3–4 are italicized.

> There is none like you, O LORD;
>   you are great, and your name is great in might.
> *Who would not fear you, O King of the nations?*
>   For that is your due.
>
> (Jer. 10:6–7a)

> There is none like you among the gods, O Lord,
>   nor are there any works like yours.
> *All the nations* you have made *shall come*

and *bow down before you, O Lord,*
and shall *glorify your name.*
For you are great and <u>do wondrous things;</u>
    you alone are God.

(Ps. 86:8–10)

In this way, John has interpreted the song of Moses in line with
the most universalistic strain in Old Testament hope: the
expectation that all the nations will come to acknowledge the
God of Israel and worship him.

The significance of this version of the song of Moses is
considerable. The effect is to shift the emphasis in the significance of the new exodus, from an event by which God
delivers his people by judging their enemies to an event which
brings the nations to acknowledge the true God. The martyrs
celebrate the victory God has won through their death and
vindication, not by praising him for their own deliverance, but
by celebrating its effect on the nations, in bringing them to
worship God. This gives a fresh significance to the use of new
exodus imagery with reference to the first stage of Christ's
work, in which by his death he ransomed a people from all the
nations to be God's own people (5:9–10). We now see that this
redemption of a special people from all the peoples is not an
end in itself, but has a further purpose: to bring all the peoples
to acknowledge and worship God. In the first stage of his work,
the Lamb's bloody sacrifice redeemed a people for God. In the
second stage, this people's participation in his sacrifice,
through martyrdom, wins all the peoples for God. This is how
God's universal kingdom comes.

It is remarkable how the meaning of this passage (15:2–4)
thus coincides exactly with that of 11:11–13, even though a
quite different set of images is used in each passage. This
confirms our interpretation of both. However, our interpretation, which recognizes a quite remarkably positive universal
hope in Revelation, must also face a difficulty. After the
passage we have just studied, Revelation continues, in
15:5–19:21, with a series of visions of the final judgment: first,
the series of seven last plagues culminating in the fall of
Babylon (15:5–16:21), then a vision of the fall of Babylon

(18:1–19:8), and finally a vision of Christ's coming to judgment and the battle of Armageddon (19:11–21).

At the first sight we might suppose that the seven last plagues are the judgments to which the song of the martyrs refers (15:4), especially since they are modelled on the plagues of Egypt. But this cannot be. They are total judgments, not even limited like the ineffective warning judgments of the seal-openings and the trumpets, certainly quite unlike the salvific judgment of 11:13. Therefore their effect is that people curse God (16:9, 11, 21). This is not only an advance on the mere failure to repent which is noticed after the sixth trumpet (9:20–1; cf. 16:9). It is the precise opposite of fearing God, giving him glory and worshipping him (11:13; 14:7; 15:4; cf. 16:9). It is true that none of the seven plagues is said to have killed anyone, but this is because the final doom of the unrepentant who curse God comes at the battle of Armageddon, at which the kings of the whole world gather with their armies (16:12–16), in alliance with the beast, to oppose Christ (17:12–14), who finally comes as king of kings to destroy them (19:19–21). The grim picture of slaughter in 19:18–19 uses strikingly universalistic language: 'the flesh of all, both free and slave, both small and great' (19:19; cf. 6:15; 13:16). This is no image of the nations coming to worship God, but of the destruction of those who refuse to worship him. The judgments of chapters 16–19 are primarily aimed at destroying the *systems* – political, economic and religious – which oppose God and his righteousness and which are symbolized by the beast, the false prophet, Babylon, and the kings of the earth. But those who support these systems, who persist in worshipping the beast, heeding neither the call to worship God nor the threat to those who worship the beast (14:6–11), evidently must perish with the evil systems with which they have identified themselves.

There is at least a tension here. The way the seven last plagues follow the martyrs' singing of the song of Moses and the Lamb was already anticipated at the end of chapter 14, in the way the positive image of the harvest of the earth was followed by the negative image of the winepress. John seems content to place indications of the universal conversion of the nations alongside references in equally universal terms to final judgment. But he is not making the kind of statements which need to be logically compatible to be valid. He is painting pictures which each portray a valid aspect of the truth. He depicts the faithful witness of the church leading to the repentance and faith of all the nations. He depicts the world which rejects their witness, unrepentant in its final adherence to the beast, necessarily subject to final judgment. The two pictures correspond to the choice presented to the nations by the proclamations of the angels in 14:6–11. It is no part of the purpose of John's prophecy to pre-empt this choice in a prediction of the *degree* of success the witness of the martyrs will have. Even if this could be known, it is not what his readers need to know. For them, the prophecy is a call not to be identified with the beast or with Babylon and to share their doom, but to bear courageously and faithfully the testimony of Jesus to the point of death. In this way they fulfil their calling to be God's special people for the salvation of all the peoples.

If this positive aspect of the prophetic future necessarily falls out of view, while the visions of final judgment take their course, it returns to prove its theological priority – and therefore eschatological ultimacy – in the vision of the New Jerusalem. The voice from the throne in 21:3 proclaims:

> Behold, the dwelling of God is with humans.
> He will dwell with them as their God;
> they will be his peoples, and God himself will be with them.[13]

In a characteristic use of the Old Testament, these words combine two sources. Ezekiel 37:27–8 reads:

> My dwelling place shall be with them [Israel]; and I will be their God, and they shall be my people. Then the nations shall know that I the LORD sanctify Israel, when my sanctuary is among them for evermore.

But this vision of God's people among the nations is taken a step further in Zechariah 2:10–11:

---

[13] There are significant variant readings in the textual tradition of this verse (including *laos* for *laoi*), but this translation is of the most probably original text.

Sing and rejoice, O daughter of Zion! For lo, I will come and dwell in your midst, says the LORD. Many nations shall join themselves to the LORD on that day, and shall be my people; and I will dwell in your midst.

As in his version of the song of Moses, John takes up the most universalistic form of the hope of the Old Testament. It will not be Israel alone that will be God's people with whom he dwells. It will not even be the eschatological Israel, redeemed from every people. Rather, as a result of the witness of the special people, all the peoples will be God's peoples (see also 21:24–6).

THE PAROUSIA

It will be useful to sum up the first two stages of Christ's work of establishing God's rule. In the first stage, by his faithful witness to death as the Passover Lamb of the new exodus, he won the comprehensive victory over all evil. The immediate result was the creation of a people, drawn from all the nations, who are already God's kingdom in the midst of opposition in this rebellious world. But this elect people is called to a role in the achievement of God's universal kingdom which is revealed by the opening of the sealed scroll and which it is the central purpose of John's prophecy to communicate to the churches. The people called from all nations are to participate in Christ's victory by bearing witness, as he did, as far as death, in a great conflict with the idolatrous power of the Roman Empire. In this way they will witness to all the nations and bring them to repentance and faith in the true God. Revelation sets side by side, without qualifying one by the other, the two possible outcomes: the conversion of the nations and their inclusion in God's kingdom or the judgment of the unrepentant nations.

This second possibility means that there is a third and final stage of Christ's work, which, like the first and second, is also described as victory – in Revelation 17:14. Although the syntactical connexion of the final words of that verse (referring to 'those with him') with the rest of the statement is not unambiguous, the meaning must be that the Lamb's followers (almost certainly the martyrs triumphant with him over death) share in his victory. They accompany him in the battle as the kings accompany the beast (17:12). They are the armies of heaven who ride with him (19:14), when he appears as the divine Warrior from heaven riding to victory (19:11). He comes as 'king of kings and lord of lords' (17:14; 19:16) to crush all political power that does not acknowledge the rule of God that he implements on earth.

But again we need the image of witness to supplement that of war in understanding Revelation's picture of the parousia. Witness to the truth is double-edged. On the one hand, it is the only means of winning people from lies and illusion to the truth. So it can convert people from the worship of the beast to the worship of the true God. But, on the other hand, witness which is rejected becomes evidence against those who reject it. Those who love lies and cling to delusion in the face of truth can only be condemned by truth. This is why Revelation characteristically joins truth to justice in speaking of God's judgments on evil (15:3; 16:7; 19:2; cf. 6:10).

While the devil and the beast reign, the earth is the sphere of deceit and illusion. Truth is seen first in heaven and then when it comes from heaven to earth. At 19:11, heaven opens and truth himself, the Word of God (19:13), rides to earth. This is the point at which the perspective of heaven prevails on earth, finally dispelling all the lies of the beast. It must finally be evident to all who has the true divine sovereignty, and so although Christ in this passage is given several names, the name which is visible for all to see, blazoned on the side of his robe is: 'Kings of kings and lord of lords' (19:16). The military imagery is controlled by judicial imagery. The sword with which he slays is the sword that comes from his mouth (19:15, 21): his word of true judgment (cf. 1:16; 2:12, 16). His eyes of flame (19:12) are those of the divine judge who sees infallibly into hearts and minds (1:14; 2:18, 23). So this is not the slaughtered Lamb turned slaughterer, but it is the witness turned judge. The 'faithful and true witness' (3:14) is now 'called faithful and true' (19:11), but not witness. His same faithfulness to the same truth now makes him the judge of those who persist in lies. Similarly, although he is not portrayed as the Lamb (but cf. 7:14), the blood of his faithful witness to death still marks him (19:13a) and qualifies him to be the Word of God in person (19:13b). So it is the truth of God, to which the Lamb and the martyrs have witnessed, which here finally prevails over those who would not be won to it, condemning them to perish with their lies (19:20). In consequence of this victory over deceit on earth, the devil himself, the source of all lies, is bound so that he may not deceive the nations (20:1–3).

With this understanding of the witness of Jesus to the truth of God, which is salvific, intended to liberate people from error, but which must in the end condemn those who reject it, it is instructive to compare John 12:46–9: exactly the same thought in an idiom rather different from Revelation's. It helps to explain why early Christians commonly understood Jesus as both Saviour now and Judge at the end, without feeling any of the incongruity modern minds often find in that combination.

THE MILLENNIUM

Mention must finally be made of the millennium, because in the theology of Revelation the millennium is to be understood in very close connexion with the parousia. This is shown by the fate of the devil, who finally shares the same fate as the beast and the false prophet, but only after a delay of a thousand years (19:20; 20:1–3, 7–10). The consequence of the parousia is the destruction of all evil, but the destruction of evil at its deepest level is portrayed not as an immediate consequence, but one delayed a thousand years. Before asking why this is, we must notice that another effect of the millennium is to separate one aspect of the last judgment (20:4) by a thousand years from the last judgment itself (20:11–13). Comparing Revelation 20 with one of its major sources, the vision of the divine judgment in Daniel 7:9, we see that the thrones of Revelation 20:4 come from Daniel 7:9, and the opening of the books in Revelation 20:11 from Daniel 7:10.

Daniel 7 concerns the destruction of the beast that has persecuted the people of God and the transference of his kingdom to the Son of Man and his people. It is this which Revelation depicts in 19:11–21 (the destruction of the beast) and 20:4–6 (the transference of the kingdom to the saints). The negative aspect of the final judgment (19:11–21), in which the beast was condemned, requires as its positive counterpart that judgment be given in favour of the martyrs, who must be vindicated and rewarded. In the contest between the beast and the witnesses of Jesus the beast appeared to triumph and the martyrs to be defeated. When the heavenly perspective finally prevails on earth, so that the truth of things becomes evident, not only must the beast be seen to be defeated, but also the martyrs must be seen to triumph. As the kings of the earth who shared the beast's usurped rule are deprived of their kingdom, so the martyrs now reign with Christ.

Thus what is said about the martyrs in 20:4–6 is strictly limited to what contrasts with the fate of the beast. Their evidence, with Christ's, has condemned him, but the divine court vindicates them. He has been thrown into the lake of fire (19:20), which is the second death (20:14), but they come to life and the second death has no power over them (20:4–6). The kingdom has been taken from him and is given to them. Now that the destroyers of the earth have been destroyed (11:18), the earth is given to Christ's people to rule with him (20:4; cf. 5:10; Dan. 7:18, 27). Life and rule – the two issues on which the contest between the martyrs and the beast had focussed – are the sole themes of 20:4–6, and they are merely asserted, without elaboration.

This shows that the theological point of the millennium is solely to demonstrate the triumph of the martyrs: that those whom the beast put to death are those who will truly live – eschatologically, and that those who contested his right to rule and suffered for it are those who will in the end rule as universally as he – and for much longer: a thousand years! Finally, to demonstrate that their triumph in Christ's kingdom is not one which evil can again reverse, that it is God's last word for good against evil, the devil is given a last chance to deceive the nations again (20:7–8). But it is no re-run of the rule of the beast. The citadel of the saints proves impregnable (20:9).

Thus John has taken from the Jewish apocalyptic tradition the notion of a temporary messianic reign on earth before the last judgment and the new creation (cf. 2 Bar. 40:3; 4 Ezra 7:28–9; b.Sanh. 99a), but he has characteristically made something different of it. He has used it to depict an essential aspect of his concept of the victory of the martyrs over the beast. He has given the image of the millennium a very specific function. But once we take the image literally – as predicting an actual period in the future history of the world – it is impossible to limit it to this function. We then have to ask all the questions which interpreters of Revelation ask about the millennium[14] but which John does not answer because they are irrelevant to the function he gives it in his symbolic universe. We have to ask: whom do the saints rule? Do they rule from heaven or on earth? How is the eschatological life of resurrection compatible with an unrenewed earth? Who are the nations Satan deceives at the end of the millennium? And so on. The millennium becomes incomprehensible once we take the image literally. But there is no more need to take it literally than to suppose that the sequences of judgments (the seal-openings, the trumpets, the bowls) are literal predictions. John no doubt expected there to be judgments, but his descriptions of them are imaginative schemes designed to depict the meaning of the judgments. John expected the martyrs to be vindicated, but the millennium depicts the meaning, rather than predicting the manner of their vindication.

[14] For the various views on the millennium which have been held during Christian history and are held today, see R. Bauckham, 'Millennium', in S. B. Ferguson and D. F. Wright, ed., *New Dictionary of Theology* (Leicester: Inter-Varsity Press, 1988), 428–30; R. G. Clouse, ed., *The Meaning of the Millennium: Four Views* (Downers Grove, Illinois: Inter-Varsity Press, 1977).

CHAPTER 5

The Spirit of prophecy

STATISTICS

Compared with references to God and Christ, references to the Spirit in Revelation are comparatively few. But it would be a mistake to conclude that in the theology of Revelation the Spirit is unimportant. As we shall see, the Spirit plays an essential role in the divine activity of establishing God's kingdom in the world.

More important than the comparative rarity of references to the Spirit is the fact that they fall into numerical patterns comparable with those we have seen to have theological significance in relation to Revelation's terms for God and Christ. References to the Spirit fall into two major categories: those which refer to 'the seven Spirits' and those which refer to 'the Spirit'. The 'seven Spirits' are peculiar to Revelation's symbolic universe. There are four references to them (1:4; 3:1; 4:5; 5:6). Four, as we have previously noticed, is the number of the world, as seven is the number of completeness. The seven Spirits are the fulness of God's power 'sent out into all the earth' (5:6). The four references to the sevenfold Spirit correspond to the seven occurrences of the fourfold phrase which designates all the peoples of the earth (5:9; 7:9; 10:11; 11:9; 13:7; 14:6; 17:15). They also correspond to the 28 (7 × 4) references to the Lamb, which, as we noted in our last chapter, indicate the worldwide scope of the Lamb's complete victory. The seven Spirits are closely associated with the victorious Lamb (5:6): the four references to them indicate that the Lamb's victory is implemented throughout the world by the fulness of divine power.

As well as these four references to 'the seven Spirits', there are also fourteen references to 'the Spirit'. Seven of these are in a category of their own: the injunction which is repeated in each of the seven messages to the churches: 'Let anyone who has an ear listen to what the Spirit is saying to the churches' (2:7, 11, 17, 29; 3:6, 13, 22). This leaves seven other references, four in the phrase 'in the Spirit' (1:10; 4:2; 17:3; 21:10), two citing words of the Spirit (14:13; 22:17), and one in the phrase 'the Spirit of prophecy' (19:10). It is notable also that the word 'prophecy' itself occurs seven times (1:3; 11:6; 19:10; 22:7, 10, 18, 19).[1]

THE SEVEN SPIRITS

The seven Spirits, called in 1:4 'the seven Spirits who are before [God's] throne', have sometimes been identified, not as the divine Spirit, but as the seven principal angels who, in Jewish angelology, stand in the presence of God in heaven (e.g. Tob. 12:15). But Revelation itself refers to these seven angels (8:2) in terms quite different from the way it refers to the seven Spirits. Moreover, although the term 'spirit' could certainly be used of angels (as frequently in the Dead Sea Scrolls), it very rarely has this meaning in early Christian literature and never in Revelation.

The seven Spirits should be understood as a symbol for the divine Spirit, which John has chosen on the basis of his exegesis of Zechariah 4:1–14, a passage which lies behind not only the four references to the seven Spirits but also the description of the two witnesses in 11:4. It seems to have been the key Old Testament passage for John's understanding of the role of the Spirit in the divine activity in the world. If we wonder why he should have attached such importance to this very obscure vision of Zechariah, the answer probably lies in the word of the Lord which he would have understood as the central message of the vision: 'Not by might, nor by power, but by my Spirit, says the LORD of hosts' (Zech. 4:6). The question to which the

---

[1] The word πνεῦμα occurs also in 11:11; 22:6, which I judge not to be references to the divine Spirit, and in 13:15; 16:13, 14; 18:2, which clearly are not.

message of Revelation is the answer was: given the apparently irresistible might and worldwide power of the beast, how is God going to establish his rule on earth? Zechariah 4:6 indicates that it will be not by worldly power like the beast's, but by the divine Spirit.

In Zechariah's vision he is shown a golden lampstand on which are seven lamps. John could not have failed to connect this with the seven-branched lampstand that stood in the holy place in the temple (cf. Exod. 25:31–40; 40:4, 24–5). Beside the lampstand are two olive trees (Zech. 4:3). As John no doubt understood the narrative, Zechariah asks first about the identity of the seven lamps (4:4–5) and then about the identity of the olive trees (4:11–13). His first question is not immediately answered directly. First he is given the oracle just quoted ('Not by might, nor by power, but by my Spirit': 4:6), followed by further words of the Lord which expand on this point (4:7–10a), and then his question is directly answered: 'These seven are the eyes of the LORD, which range through the whole earth' (4:10b). John evidently took this sequence to mean that the seven lamps symbolize the seven eyes of the LORD, which are the divine Spirit. We postpone for the moment the question of the identity of the olive trees.

In John's vision of heaven he sees seven lamps burning before the divine throne, which he identifies as the seven Spirits (Rev. 4:5). Since the heavenly sanctuary was understood as the model on which the earthly sanctuary was constructed and in John's visions it therefore contains the most important contents of the earthly sanctuary (cf. 8:3–5; 11:19; 15), these seven lamps correspond to the seven lamps which burned 'before the LORD' (Exod. 40:25) in the earthly sanctuary. They are the lamps of Zechariah's vision. No doubt a lampstand is presupposed, but it is probably significant that John does not mention it: the lampstands he mentions are on earth (1:12–13, 20; 2:1, 5; 11:4). As the seven lamps before the throne in heaven, the seven Spirits belong to the divine being. This is why the reference to them in the 'trinitarian' blessing of 1:4–5a is also to 'the seven Spirits who are before his throne'.

But if these references associate the seven Spirits with God, in 5:6 they are very closely associated with the Lamb, who is said to have 'seven horns and seven eyes, which are the seven Spirits of God sent out into all the earth'. The echo of Zechariah 4:10b is clear. In Revelation the eyes of Yahweh are also the eyes of the Lamb. This has an exegetical basis in Zechariah 3:9, where John would have taken the 'stone with seven eyes' to refer to Christ and the seven eyes to be the same as those of Zechariah 4:10b.

Probably Revelation 5:6 identifies the seven Spirits with *both* the seven horns *and* the seven eyes of the Lamb. It is important to realize that the eyes of Yahweh in the Old Testament indicate not only his ability to see what happens throughout the world, but also his ability to act powerfully wherever he chooses. The message of the prophet Hanani in 2 Chronicles 16:7–9, which makes verbal allusion to Zechariah 4:10b (16:9: 'the eyes of the LORD range throughout the entire earth'), clearly understands this verse, as John did, in connexion with Zechariah 4:6 ('Not by might, nor by power, but by my Spirit'). Hanani rebukes king Asa for having relied on the power of an army instead of on Yahweh, whose eyes range throughout the world to help those who rely on him.[2] This connexion between God's all-seeing eyes and his power John makes explicit by adding seven horns, the well-known symbol of strength, to the seven eyes. Probably he noticed that in Zechariah the power of Yahweh is opposed to the power of the nations inimical to God's people, symbolized by four horns (Zech. 1:18–21). Similarly, in Revelation, the seven horns of the Lamb are the divine power set against the horns of the dragon and the beasts (Rev. 12:3; 13:1, 11; 17:12–13). The crucial question, however, is the nature of this divine power.

The seven horns and the seven eyes belong to the description of the Lamb when he first appears in Revelation: as the slaughtered Lamb who has conquered (5:5–6). They represent the power of his victory. The seven Spirits are sent out into all the earth to make his victory effective throughout the world. While God himself, the One who sits on the throne, dwells in

[2] Cf. the very similar passage Ps. 33:13–19; cf. also Ps. 34:15; Sir. 34:15–16.

heaven, not yet on earth, and while the Lamb, victorious through his death on earth, now shares his Father's throne in heaven, the seven Spirits are the presence and power of God on earth, bringing about God's kingdom by implementing the Lamb's victory throughout the world. Thus John's understanding of the seven Spirits corresponds broadly to the common early Christian understanding of the Holy Spirit's relation to God and to Christ, as the divine power which is now the Spirit of Christ, the manner of the exalted Christ's presence in the world and of the present effect of Christ's past work.[3] It remains to be seen whether the seven Spirits are also related to the church in the way that early Christians commonly envisaged the Spirit.

The seven Spirits are related to the two witnesses of 11:3–13, not explicitly but via the allusions to Zechariah 4. The two olive trees of Zechariah's vision are said to be 'the two anointed ones [literally: 'sons of oil'] who stand by the Lord of the whole earth' (4:14). Revelation's two witnesses are 'the two olive trees and the two lampstands that stand before the Lord of the earth' (11:4). If 'the two olive trees' have a significance for John more than simply as a way of referring to Zechariah's vision, it is probably that the two are prophets (cf. 11:3, 10), anointed with the oil of the Spirit. But in identifying them with two lampstands, he has modified the symbolism of Zechariah's vision. He must mean that they are lampstands bearing the lamps which are the seven Spirits, though since he has chosen to have only two witnesses, according to the requirement for valid witness, and therefore only two lampstands, he cannot refer to the seven Spirits without confusing the imagery intolerably. Nevertheless, the implication is clear that the seven Spirits are the power of the church's prophetic witness to the world, symbolized by the ministry of the two witnesses. The universality of this witness is suggested by the phrase from Zechariah, that they 'stand before the Lord of the earth', which also relates their universal witness to God's or Christ's lordship of the world. It is therefore through their prophetic

---

[3] See, e.g., Y. Congar, *I Believe in the Holy Spirit*, vol. 1 (New York: Seabury Press; London: Geoffrey Chapman, 1983), chapter 2.

witness that the seven Spirits are sent out into all the earth. The horns and the eyes of the Lamb are the power and discernment of their prophetic witness, which is their faithfulness to the witness Jesus bore. Through this witness the seven Spirits make the victory of the Lamb effective universally.

Similarly the seven churches are represented as seven gold lampstands (1:12, 20; 2:1). Zechariah's single lampstand, holding seven lamps, is divided into seven lampstands to correspond to the seven individual churches of Asia, which, as the number of completeness, in turn represent all the churches of the world. This makes it possible for the seven Spirits to be explicitly mentioned in connexion with the churches. Christ is called 'the one who has the seven Spirits of God and the seven stars' (3:1). Since the seven stars are the angels of the seven churches (1:16, 20), there is a hint of some kind of correspondence of the seven Spirits to the seven churches. But it can be no more than a hint, while it is not yet explained in what the 'conquering' required of all the churches consists. Only when the churches' role of prophetic witness to the world is explained (beginning in 11:3–13), can the hint be understood. It is as the lamps on the seven golden lampstands that the seven Spirits are sent out into all the earth.

Thus it could be said that the seven Spirits as the divine power released into the whole world by the victory of Christ's sacrifice are the power of divine truth: the power of the church's faithful witness to the truth of God and his righteousness against the idolatries and injustices of the world under the sway of the beast. As the power of truth the seven Spirits can be represented both as eyes (for discernment) and horns (for power). It is instructive to compare the seven Spirits, in this respect, with their counterpart in the satanic trinity. If the dragon, who gives his throne and authority to the beast (13:2), is the satanic parody of God as the One who sits on the throne, and the beast, who recovers from a mortal wound (13:3), is a parody of the slaughtered Lamb, it might seem that the false prophet (as the second beast is called in 16:13; 19:20) must be a parody of the seven Spirits. But this is not quite the case. He corresponds not to the seven Spirits as such, nor, as is sometimes claimed, to the Christian prophets as such, but to the two witnesses, who represent the church's prophetic witness inspired by the seven Spirits. His prophetic activity relates to the whole world (13:12–17; 16:13–14), as does that of the two witnesses. He performs signs (13:13–14; 19:20), as they do (11:6). He makes the world worship the beast (13:12), which is tantamount to worshipping the dragon (13:4), just as the career of the two witnesses brings the world to worship God (11:13), including no doubt the worship of Jesus, which in Revelation is tantamount to the worship of God. Whereas the two witnesses do all this by the power of truth, the false prophet does it by deceit (19:20) and coercion (13:15–17). But the very killings with which he enforces his lies are the Christian martyrdoms which manifest the power of truth. This is how Revelation understands the contrast: 'Not by might, nor by power, but by my Spirit' (Zech. 4:6).

THE SPIRIT OF CHRISTIAN PROPHECY IN THE CHURCHES

The seven Spirits represent the fulness of the divine Spirit in relation to God, to Christ and to the church's mission to the whole world. This is what distinguishes the references to the seven Spirits from the references simply to the Spirit. The latter concern the activity of the Spirit through the Christian prophets within the churches.[4] We shall briefly consider these references before enquiring into the relationship between the two ways of speaking of the Spirit.

All fourteen of the references to the Spirit concern, in various ways, the Spirit's inspiration of John's prophecy, the book of Revelation itself. Only one of these cases (19:10) also has a wider reference to Christian prophecy in general, though we can assume that in all cases the activity attributed to the Spirit could be paralleled in Christian prophecy other than John's.

There are four references to John's reception of visionary

---

[4] On this, cf. D. Hill, 'Prophecy and Prophets in the Revelation of St John', *NTS* 18 (1971–2), 401–18; and *New Testament Prophecy* (London: Marshall, Morgan & Scott, 1979), chapter 3.

revelation 'in the Spirit'.[5] Twice he says that he 'was in the Spirit' (1:10; 4:2), twice that the angel 'carried him away in the Spirit' (or: 'by means of the Spirit': 17:3; 21:10). Parallels to these expressions in other literature[6] make it clear that the reference is not to John's human spirit (as in NRSV and some other translations) but to the divine Spirit as the agent of visionary experience. The two references to transportation by the Spirit (17:3; 21:10), in which John is taken to a new visionary location, are based especially on a common formula in Ezekiel (3:12, 14, etc.), who is the Old Testament prophet on whom John most modelled his accounts of his own prophetic experience and claims. The four references are strategically placed: at the two beginnings of John's whole vision, on earth among the churches (1:10) and in heaven in the divine throne-room (4:2), and at the beginnings of the two parallel visions of Babylon (17:3) and the New Jerusalem (21:10). The effect is not merely to associate parts of John's visionary experience with the Spirit, but to attribute the whole of it to the agency of the divine Spirit.

The Spirit enables John to receive the visions in which he is given his prophetic revelations. The Spirit thus performs a role distinct from the chain of revelation by which the content of John's prophecy comes to him from God (God – Christ – angel – John: 1:1; cf. 22:16). The Spirit does not give the content of the revelation, but the visionary experience which enables John to receive the revelation. These references to the Spirit do constitute a claim to real visionary experience underlying the book, though this does not mean that the book is simply a transcript of that experience. The book is far too complex and elaborate a literary composition for that to be possible, and much of its meaning is embodied in purely literary form. Whatever John's visionary experiences were, he has transmuted them, by a long process of reflection, study and literary

---

[5] For fuller discussion of these references, see R. Bauckham, 'The Role of the Spirit in the Apocalypse', *EQ* 52 (1980), 66–83; revised version (chapter 5) in Bauckham, *The Climax of Prophecy*.

[6] Ezek. 3:12, 14; 8:3; 11:1, 24; 37:1; 43:5; Bel 36 (Theod.); 2 Bar. 6:3; Hermas, *Vis.* 1:3; 5:1; Josephus, *Ant.* 4.118; Pseudo-Philo, *L.A.B.* 28:6; cf. Did. 11:7–9; Polycrates, ap. Eusebius, *Hist. Eccl.* 5.24.2; Melito, ap. Eusebius, *Hist. Eccl.* 5.34.5.

composition, into a literary work which communicates their message to others. But even more than a claim to visionary experience, these four references to the Spirit are a claim that his prophecy is divinely inspired. They complement the claim that the revelation came from God and reinforce the very strong claim to divine authority (cf. 22:18 19) by which John places his work in the same category as the canonical prophets – or gives it in a certain sense even a higher status, as the final prophetic revelation in which the whole tradition of biblical prophecy culminates (cf. 10:7).

Besides these references to the Spirit as the agent of visionary experience, others are to the Spirit as inspiring prophetic oracles. Each of the messages to the seven churches has, as its final or penultimate component, the 'proclamation formula', calling for attention to what has been said: 'Let anyone who has an ear listen to what the Spirit is saying to the churches.' This is no doubt modelled on the formula which is prominent in the tradition of the sayings of Jesus (Mark 4:9, 23, etc.) and deliberately recalls that formula, for the seven messages are the words of the exalted Christ. Each begins, 'Thus says … ', followed by a description of Christ. Thus what the Spirit says is what the exalted Christ says. He inspires the prophetic oracles in which the prophet John speaks Christ's words to the churches. No doubt this is also implicitly the case with oracles in which the exalted Christ directly addresses the churches but where the Spirit is not explicitly mentioned (16:15; 22:7, 12–13, 16, 20).

However, the Spirit's words are not always those of the exalted Christ. In the two other instances in which Revelation explicitly attributes words to the Spirit they are not the words of Christ. In 14:13b they are the Spirit's response to the words of the heavenly voice John hears. As John obeys the command to write the beatitude (14:13a), the Spirit inspiring him adds an emphatic endorsement of it. In 22:17a, the prayer, 'Come!', attributed to the Spirit and the Bride, is addressed to Christ, as the response to Christ's promise to come in 22:12. (The same promise and response recur in 22:20.) The meaning of 'the Spirit and the Bride' cannot be that the Spirit here inspires the prayer of the whole Christian community, for the prayer of the Spirit and the Bride is followed by an invitation to Christians who hear it to add their own prayer to it: 'And let anyone who hears say, "Come!"' This formula is a parallel to that in the seven messages: 'Let anyone who has an ear hear ... ' The latter is the appropriate response to a Spirit-inspired prophecy, the former to a Spirit-inspired prayer. So we are to think of Christian prophets (or simply John himself) praying in the Spirit and so giving a lead to the prayers of the whole church. What the Spirit prays through the Christian prophets is what the church in her eschatological purity, ready for the coming of her husband the Lamb (cf. 19:7–8; 21:2), should pray, and so the prayer is ascribed to 'the Spirit and the Bride'.

Thus in all these instances, as well as in the more general statement of 19:10, which does not give specific words of the Spirit, 'the Spirit' indicates the inspired utterance of Christian prophets, principally, in this context, John himself. The Spirit of prophecy brings the words of the exalted Christ to his people on earth, endorses on earth the words of heavenly revelations, and directs the prayers of the churches to their heavenly Lord. The Spirit in these references is the divine presence on earth, not in heaven, but unlike the seven Spirits which are 'sent out into all the earth' (5:6), the Spirit's sphere is the churches, where he inspires the ministry of the Christian prophets to the rest of the community.

PROPHECY AS THE WITNESS OF JESUS

We have seen that the distinction between 'the seven Spirits' and 'the Spirit' is that the former represent the fulness of the divine Spirit, sent out from the presence of God, through Christ's victory, in a mission to the whole world which is the prophetic witness of the churches to the world, whereas 'the Spirit' refers to Christian prophecy within the churches. 'The Spirit' speaks through the prophets to the churches; 'the seven Spirits' address the whole world through the churches. However, this does not mean that the two are unconnected. The notion of prophecy connects them. Prophecy as the

Spirit's message through prophets to the churches is designed to prepare and to enable the churches to bear their prophetic witness to the world, inspired by the Spirit.

A key statement is in 19:10: 'the testimony of Jesus is the Spirit of prophecy'. Difficult as it is, this must mean that when the Spirit inspires prophecy, its content is the witness of Jesus. In this context, the prophecy in question (and the only way Revelation uses the noun) is prophecy communicated by the Christian prophets to the churches. Most immediately, it is John's own prophecy, the book of Revelation (cf. 1:3; 22:7, 18–19). So it is relevant to notice that the content of Revelation is said to be the witness of Jesus, as well as the word of God (1:2), attested by Jesus himself (22:20) as well as by the angel who communicates it to John (22:16) and by John himself (1:2). But if the content of Christian prophecy, and Revelation in particular, is 'the witness of Jesus', and so the Christian prophets in their ministry to the churches can be called 'those who hold the testimony of Jesus' (the probable meaning of 19:10), it is by no means only the Christian prophets who witness as Jesus did. All Christians, in their witness to the world, are those who 'hold the testimony of Jesus' (12:17; cf. 6:9; 12:11; 17:6; 20:4). Moreover, the link between the witness of Jesus and the word of God is found both in reference to Revelation itself as prophecy (1:2) and in reference to the Christian martyrs (6:9; 20:4).

Revelation clearly distinguishes between prophets and other Christians (11:18; 16:6; 18:20, 24; 22:9). But it can use the same terms for the prophecy given by the prophets to the churches and for the witness given by faithful Christians in general to the world. Only in the story of the two witnesses is the latter actually equated with prophecy (11:3, 6, 10). This does not mean that every Christian could be called a prophet, as the two witnesses themselves are, because the two witnesses are not, as it were, paradigmatic Christians, but symbolic individuals standing for the whole church. Each Christian is not a lamp-stand. Only a church is symbolized by a lampstand. It is not primarily each individual Christian's witness to the world, but the church's witness to the world which is depicted as prophetic in 11:3–13. Of course, every Christian is called on to participate in that witness, but this stops a little short of saying that each Christian is a prophet. It is relevant to note that, although witness itself, in Revelation, appears to be always verbal and although verbal witness is certainly required of every Christian when the circumstances demand it, it is also closely connected with obedience to the commandments of God (12:17).[7]

This suggests that the reason why Revelation extends the vocation of prophecy to the church as a whole is probably not because of the thought that all Christians, as members of the eschatological community on which the Spirit has been poured out (cf. Acts 2:17), are endowed with the Spirit of prophecy and so are actually (Acts 19:6), or at least potentially, prophets. This idea apparently had some influence in early Christianity, but the thought in Revelation is different. It is connected with the idea of the church's newly revealed role of confronting the idolatry of Rome in a prophetic conflict, like that of Moses with Pharaoh and his magicians or of Elijah with Jezebel and her prophets of Baal, and in the power of the Spirit of prophecy winning the nations to the worship of the true God. The fact that the revelation of this role is the central content of John's own prophecy accounts for the specially close correlation between the way he describes his own witness as prophet (1:2) and the way he describes the witness of Christians to the world. It also accounts for the virtual impossibility of deciding whether, in 10:11, John is commanded to prophesy *to* the nations, so that his own prophetic role is paradigmatic for the churches' prophetic witness to the nations, or to prophesy *about* the nations, in a prophecy to the churches enabling them to prophesy to the nations.

We can return to 19:10 and consider the whole verse. When John offers to worship the angel, he is told: 'You must not do that! I am a fellow servant with you and your brothers and sisters who hold the testimony of Jesus. Worship God! For the testimony of Jesus is the Spirit of prophecy.' Probably the final

---

[7] Note also especially 14:12, which is another variation on the language of 6:9; 12:11, 17; 14:12; 20:4, but uniquely does not refer to verbal witness.

sentence is more than an appended note explaining what the 'testimony of Jesus' is and therefore that John's brothers and sisters who hold it are the prophets. It is more integrally connected with the point of the angel's words. With the words 'Worship God!' the angel directs John back to the central theme of all prophecy and certainly of the revelation that is to be the theme of John's prophecy. To distinguish the one true God and his righteousness from idolatry and its evils is the theme of true prophecy. It is the theme of the witness of Jesus, certainly as that witness must be continued by his followers in the pagan cities of Asia. But, once again, it is equally the theme of John's prophecy and the theme of the prophetic witness which his prophecy calls on the churches to bear to the nations.

When the incident is repeated, the angel's words are: 'You must not do that! I am a fellow servant with you and your brothers and sisters the prophets, and with those who keep the words of this book. Worship God!' (22:9) Here the fellow servants are extended to include all faithful Christians who heed and obey John's prophecy along with the prophets themselves. This is an acknowledgment that the role to which Revelation calls all Christians is, in essence, the same as that of prophets: bearing the witness of Jesus, remaining faithful in word and deed to the one true God and his righteousness.

THE PROPHETIC MESSAGES TO THE CHURCHES

We have seen that there are close links between, on the one hand, prophecy addressed to the churches and, on the other, the churches' prophetic witness to the world. Both are the witness of Jesus and the word of God. Both concern the truth of the one God and his righteousness. Both are inspired by the divine Spirit as the power of God's truth in the world. Both concern the establishment of God's kingdom in the world. Prophecy within the churches equips the churches to fulfil their prophetic ministry to the world, which is their indispensable role in the coming of God's kingdom, the task to which it is the function of Revelation to call them.

Having understood this connexion between prophecy to the

churches and the churches' witness to the world, we can see more clearly the significance of the seven messages to the churches within the overall purpose of Revelation. Several features of them are worth noticing:

First, we may notice a dominant concern with truth in the messages. The churches are commended for *not denying* (2:13; 3:8). They are reproved for having a false reputation which hides the truth of their condition (3:1) or for deceiving themselves about their condition (3:17). The prophet Jezebel is charged with deceit (2:20). There are the false apostles, who say they are apostles but are not (2:2), just as there are those who lie, saying they are Jews but are not (2:9; 3:9). In every message, with its opening 'I know ... ', Jesus Christ addresses the churches as the one who knows the real truth of their condition, despite misleading appearances (2:9), false reputations (3:1), false confidence (3:17) and slanders (2:9). Those who were probably claiming that outward participation in idolatry was permissible because what counts is only one's inner integrity, he reminds that he sees the truth of hearts and minds (2:23). He walks among the lampstands, observing their real condition (2:1), and his eyes of flame penetrate the hidden truths of motives, thoughts and feelings (2:18). Thus the function of prophecy addressed to the churches is to expose the uncomfortable truth, just as the two witnesses torment the inhabitants of the earth by bringing home to them their sin (11:10).

Secondly, when Christ, in his relentless knowledge of the truth, has something against a church, the consequence is the alternative: repentance or judgment (2:5, 16; 3:3, 19). It is the same alternative with which the churches' witness confronts the world (11:3; 14:6–11). (And notice how 14:12 indicates that the churches themselves are not beyond needing to heed the alternative presented to the world in 14:6–11.)

Thirdly, Christ in his exposure of the truth of the churches appears in the role of 'the faithful and true witness', and 'the Amen' (3:14), that is, the divine truthfulness (Isa. 65:16). These titles appear at the head of the message to the church at Laodicea, probably not because they have more relevance to that church than to the others, but because Laodicea is the last of the seven. Like the description of Christ at the head of the first message, to Ephesus (2:1), they relate to Christ's knowledge of all the churches. They characterize him as the one who gives truthful evidence. Those who accept his evidence against them repent. It proves salvific. To those who reject it, the evidence itself becomes their condemnation. The witness becomes the judge (cf. Jer. 42:5 with Rev. 3:14). In imagery which anticipates the description of the parousia (19:15), he threatens to make war against them with the sword of his mouth (2:16), which is his truthful word of witness and, consequently, condemnation.

The role of prophecy as the witness of Jesus to the churches is thus entirely parallel to the witness of the churches, bearing the witness of Jesus, to the world. Judgment at the parousia threatens the churches (2:16; 3:3; cf. 16:15) no less than the world. Prophecy warns of that judgment with salvific intent, just as does the churches' witness to the world. And so there is no reason to suppose that the significant dictum, 'I reprove and discipline those whom I love' (3:19), applies only to Christ's reproof of the churches, and not also to his churches' witness to the world.

Fourthly, the domestic problems within the churches in part parallel Revelation's depiction of the world ruled by the devil and the beasts. The complacent affluence of the Laodicean Christians (3:17) is reminiscent of Babylon's exploitative self-indulgence (cf. 18:7). The idolizing of material prosperity characteristic of Rome here characterizes a whole church. Their repentance of this will be equivalent to coming out of Babylon, as God's people are urged to do, renouncing her sins lest they share her judgment (18:4).

Even closer is the link between Jezebel and the Nicolaitans, on the one hand, and the enemies of God's kingdom, on the other. Idolatry and fornication (2:14, 20) are not only characteristic evils of pagan society in general (9:20–1; cf. 21:8; 22:15): they are also the dominant characteristics respectively of the beast (chapter 13) and Babylon (chapter 17). What the Nicolaitans and Jezebel are urging is not some minor accommodation to the ways of the pagan society Christians have to live in, but complicity in that denial of the true God and his righteousness which characterizes the forces of evil incarnate in the Roman system. No wonder Jezebel is said to 'deceive' Christians (2:20) – a word used elsewhere in Revelation only of the devil, the false prophet and Babylon (12:9; 13:14; 18:23; 19:20; 20:3, 8, 10).

The point is made also by wordplay. The name of the Nicolaitans, followers of Nicolaus, which means 'conquer the people', alludes to Revelation's keyword 'conquer' (*nikaō*). Their teaching made it possible for Christians to be successful in pagan society, but this was the beast's success, a real conquest of the saints, winning them to his side, rather than the only apparent conquest he achieved by putting them to death. Hence the name Nicolaus is aptly explained by that of Balaam (2:14), the Old Testament false prophet who destroyed many of the Israelites by his plan to lure them into idolatry and fornication (Num. 25). With reference to this event, Jewish exegesis explained the name Balaam as meaning 'destroy the people' (b. Sanh. 105a).

Here we may also mention 'those who say they are Jews but are not' (2:8; 3:9), because they are virtually a domestic problem for churches with largely Jewish Christian leaders and members. Their estrangement from the synagogue was probably only recently complete as the non-Christian Jewish congregations disowned them, and even sometimes, it seems, denounced them to the authorities. Because the language about the non-Christian Jews (2:8; 3:9) now sounds offensively and dangerously anti-Semitic – and would be, if repeated outside its original context – it is important to recognize here an intra-Jewish dispute. This is not the Gentile church claiming to supersede Judaism, but a rift like that between the temple establishment and the Qumran community, who denounced their fellow-Jews as 'an assembly of deceit and a congregation of Belial' (1QH 2:22).

Moreover, it is not because they are not Christians that Revelation calls some non-Christian Jews in Smyrna and Philadelphia a 'synagogue of Satan'. It is because they 'slander', i.e. lay false accusations, which is the activity of the devil (*diabolos* means 'one who makes false accusations') and Satan (12:9; Satan means 'accuser' and by this period, when the reference is to the devil, it means 'the one who makes false accusations'). It also links them with the beast, who blasphemes (slanders) not only God but also his people (13:6). By denouncing Christians to the authorities, claiming that Jewish Christians are not Jews and so should not enjoy the legal status of Judaism as a religion, they aid and abet the beast's opposition to the worship of the true God. It is their own statement about Jewish Christians – that they 'say they are Jews but are not' – that Revelation turns against them. (Using Revelation's own conceptuality, it would have to be said of later Christians who played the beast's role against Jews, that they say they are Christians but are not.) In its context, the polemic against non-Christian Jews is an instance of the way the issues of the great conflict between the beast and the witnesses of Jesus already impinge on the largely more domestic concerns of the seven messages.

Clearly a church which listens to the Nicolaitans or imitates Babylon cannot bear faithful witness to the truth and righteousness of God. The churches must be exposed to the power of divine truth in the Spirit's words of prophecy, if they are to be the lampstands from which the seven Spirits can shine the light of truth into the world.

Finally, however, all seven messages end with encouragement and eschatological promise. Whether a church's need is for repentance or simply for endurance, all are invited to 'conquer' so that they may inherit the eschatological promises. The Spirit's prophetic ministry is both to expose the truth in this world of deceit and ambiguity, and to point to the eschatological age when the truth of all things will come to light. To live faithfully and courageously according to the truth of God now requires a vision of that eschatological future. This the Spirit gives, first in terms adapted to the situation of each church in each of the seven messages, then much more fully in the great climax of John's whole visionary revelation: the vision of the New Jerusalem, to which we turn in our next chapter.

CHAPTER 6

The New Jerusalem

THE CITIES OF REVELATION

The Christian world of the book of Revelation, like that of much of the New Testament, is a world of cities. The readers to whom the book is addressed lived in seven of the great cities of Asia Minor.[1] Most readers to whom it subsequently passed would also have lived in cities. Jewish Christians, like John and many of his readers, lived, both geographically and symbolically, between Jerusalem and Rome. And since this was also a world in which cities were commonly personified as women, Rome appears in Revelation, not as the goddess Roma, the form in which she was worshipped in the cities of Asia, but as 'the great whore' (17:1). She is also called Babylon the great city, after the Old Testament city which destroyed Jerusalem and in which Jerusalem's citizens lived in exile. Babylon is the city of Rome, built on seven hills (17:9), but she also represents the corrupting influence which Rome had on all the cities of her empire. She is 'Babylon the great, mother of whores' – who are presumably the other cities, like those of Asia, who share in her luxury and her evil. When she falls, so do 'the cities of the nations' (16:19) – presumably including Ephesus, Smyrna, Pergamum and the rest.

But if Babylon is the actual city of Rome, Jerusalem is not the actual city which the Romans had captured and sacked some time before Revelation was written. There are, indeed, two Jerusalems in Revelation. There is the New Jerusalem

[1] On the cities, see especially C. J. Hemer, *The Letters to the Seven Churches of Asia in their Local Setting* (*JSNTSS* 11; Sheffield: *JSOT* Press, 1986).

126

which comes down from heaven in the new creation. Like the harlot Babylon, the New Jerusalem is both a woman and a city: the bride and the wife of the Lamb (19:7; 21:2, 9) and 'the holy city the New Jerusalem' (21:2), 'the city of my God' (3:12). Babylon and the New Jerusalem are the contrasting pair of women-cities which dominates the later chapters of Revelation. But as well as the New Jerusalem of the future, there is also 'the holy city' of 11:2 and the heavenly woman of 12:1–6, 13–17. The city of 11:2 is not the earthly Jerusalem, in which Revelation shows no interest, and 11:1–2 does not allude to the fall of Jerusalem in AD 70, when the sanctuary in the temple was certainly not protected from the Roman armies.[2] John is here reinterpreting Daniel's prophecies of the desecration of the temple (Dan. 8:9–14; 11:31; 12:11) and perhaps also the prophecies in the Gospels, dependent on Daniel, which prophesied the fall of Jerusalem (Matt. 24:15; Mark 13:14; Luke 21:20–4). He is reinterpreting them to refer to the persecution of the church in the symbolic three-and-a-half year period of the church's conflict with the Roman Empire. The holy city trampled by the Gentiles is the faithful church in its suffering and martyrdom at the hands of the beast. The sanctuary with its worshippers is the hidden presence of God to those who worship him in the churches. In the midst of persecution they are kept spiritually safe, just as Christ promised the church at Philadelphia to 'keep' them from 'the hour of trial that is coming on the whole world' (3:10). They would suffer and die, but be kept spiritually safe. The little prophecy about the temple and the city in 11:1–2 corresponds to the spiritual immunity of the two witnesses (11:5) and their martyrdom (11:7–8). The holy city trampled by the Gentiles is wherever the witnesses lie dead in the street of the great city (11:8).

For the same period in which the sanctuary is protected, in which the holy city is trampled and the witnesses prophesy (11:1–3), the heavenly woman who has given birth to the Messiah is kept safe in the wilderness (12:6, 13–16), while the dragon, frustrated in his pursuit of her, turns his attacks onto

---

[2] For a detailed discussion of Rev. 11:1–2, see chapter 9 ('The Conversion of the Nations'), in Bauckham, *The Climax of Prophecy*.

her children (12:13–17). Her refuge in the wilderness is an alternative symbol for the same spiritual safety of the church in persecution as is depicted by the protection of the sanctuary in 11:1–2. She is kept safe while the beast rules and puts her children to death (13:5–7). She is the mother of Jesus and of Christians – Eve and Mary, Israel, Zion and the church all combined in an image of the spiritual essence of the covenant people of God.[3] She is the female figure corresponding to the holy city of 11:2.

Thus the New Jerusalem of the future, the bride of the Lamb, has both a forerunner in the present and an opposite in the present. The forerunner is the holy city, mother Zion. The opposite is Babylon, the great whore. But while Babylon is 'the great city that rules over the kings of the earth' (17:18), the holy city exists only in hiddenness and contradiction. While it resembles the New Jerusalem in its holiness, it contrasts sharply with the unchallenged glory of the New Jerusalem which the kings of the earth will honour (21:24). And while the New Jerusalem contrasts with Babylon in her evil, she resembles Babylon in splendour and universal dominion.

Whether they were Jews or Gentiles, most of John's readers were used to belonging to a city. Most citizens of the great cities of the province of Asia would have thought it possible to be fully human only in the public life of a city. For those of John's readers who had the social status and affluence sufficient to participate in this public life – and probably many of them did – the most difficult and alien aspect of Christianity would have been the extent to which it required them to dissociate and to distance themselves from this public life, because of the idolatry and immorality bound up with it. There is plenty of evidence in the seven messages to the churches to show how disinclined many of them were to do this. Not only a comfortable life, participating in the prosperity of the cities' economic life, was at stake, though this was a major factor. There was also the need to belong to the civic community, with its rituals of identity and civic pride. And in the first century AD this was

---

[3] Cf. J. Sweet, *Revelation* (London: SCM Press, 1979), 194–6.

inseparable from the public and official enthusiasm for their connexion with Rome which the cities of Asia displayed. Of course, for the poor among John's readers belonging to a city and to the Roman Empire would have had more ambivalent, though not always merely negative, connotations.

Jewish Christians may have felt their identity to depend less on participation in the life of the cities.[4] As diaspora Jews they were used to a double loyalty – to their adopted city and to the city they still looked to as their national and religious centre: Jerusalem. As a symbolic centre, a spiritual alternative to Rome, Jerusalem was of great importance to diaspora Jews, even after AD 70. But Jewish Christians at Smyrna and Philadelphia were being disowned by the Jewish community, and in any case, however Jewish Christians felt about Jerusalem before AD 70, most of them probably took the destruction of the temple to mark the end of Jerusalem's earthly significance. It was a definitive divine judgment. But it deprived them of a city to belong to.

We recall that part of the strategy of Revelation, in creating a symbolic world for its readers to enter, was to redirect their imaginative response to the world. If they were to dissociate themselves from Babylon and its corrupting influence on their own cities, they needed not only to be shown Roman civilization in a different light from the way its own propaganda portrayed it; they also needed an alternative. If they were – metaphorically – to 'come out of' Babylon (18:4), they needed somewhere to go, another city to belong to. If they were to resist the powerful allurements of Babylon, they needed an alternative and greater attraction. Since Babylon is the great city that rules over the kings of the earth (17:18), even over the earthly Jerusalem, this alternative could belong only to the eschatological future. It is God's alternative city: the New Jerusalem that comes down from heaven. It belongs to the future, but through John's vision it exercises its attraction already. On its great high mountain in the future (21:10), it

---

[4] On the (varied) extent of Jewish involvement in the life of the cities of Asia Minor, see P. Trebilco, *Jewish Communities in Asia Minor* (SNTSMS 69; Cambridge University Press, 1991).

towers above the impressive citadel of Pergamum where Satan
had his throne (2:13) and even above the seven mountains on
which Babylon was built (17:9). Its radiance, which is the
glory of God, already attracts people to it – even, through the
church's witness, the nations and their rulers (21:24). John's
readers may not enter it yet, but they may anticipate a place in
it (3:12, 22:14, 19), and belong already to the Bride of the
Lamb (19:7–8; 22:17), whose marriage to him will be the city's
arrival on earth(21:2).

Thus, because their spiritual centre in the present is hidden
and contradicted (11:1–2), while the splendour and power of
Babylon dominate the world, including the life of their own
cities, John's readers need the vision of a centre in the eschatological future towards which they may live. It has to be
presented as the alternative to Babylon, and so the visions of
the harlot city Babylon (17:1–19:10) and the Lamb's bride the
New Jerusalem (21:9–22:9) form a structural pair in the latter
part of the book. They both play on the ancient mythic ideal of
the city as the place where human community lives in security
and prosperity with the divine in its midst. Babylon represents
the perversion of this ideal, what it comes to when, instead of
the true God, humanity's self-deification is the heart of the city.
All the proud, God-defying, tyrannical and oppressive cities
and states of the Old Testament contribute to the picture:
Babel, Sodom, Egypt, Tyre, Babylon, Edom. The Babylon of
Revelation sums up and surpasses them all. But the echoes of
the past are tailored to the reality of the present: John's readers
would recognize well enough contemporary Rome in her true
colours. Conversely, the New Jerusalem represents the true
fulfilment of the ideal of the city, a city truly worth belonging
to. It takes up the ideal to which the earthly Jerusalem aspired
but surpasses her in an eschatological excess already to be
found in the visions of the Old Testament prophets. The fall of
Babylon, which occupies so much of Revelation, is what
human opposition to God must come to, but it is not celebrated
for its own sake. Babylon must fall so that the New Jerusalem
may replace her. Her satanic parody of the ideal of the city
must give way to the divine reality. But John hopes that, before

this happens, not only his readers but even, through them, the nations, may be won from the deceitful charms of Babylon to the genuine attractions of the New Jerusalem.

For this reason, the two visions of Babylon and the New Jerusalem are replete with parallels and contrasts between the two.[5] A list of some of the major ways in which the New Jerusalem is presented as God's alternative to Babylon will illustrate the point:

(1) The chaste bride, the wife of the Lamb (21:2,9)
   v. the harlot with whom the kings of the earth fornicate (17:2)

(2) Her splendour is the glory of God (21:11–21)
   v. Babylon's splendour from exploiting her empire (17:4; 18:12–13, 16)

(3) The nations walk by her light, which is the glory of God (21:24)
   v. Babylon's corruption and deception of the nations (17:2; 18:3, 23; 19:2)

(4) The kings of the earth bring their glory into her (i.e. their worship and submission to God: 21:24)
   v. Babylon rules over the kings of the earth (17:18)

(5) They bring the glory and honour of the nations into her (i.e. glory to God: 21:26)
   v. Babylon's luxurious wealth extorted from all the world (18:12–17)

(6) Uncleanness, abomination and falsehood are excluded (21:27)
   v. Babylon's abominations, impurities, deceptions (17:4, 5; 18:23)

(7) The water of life and the tree of life for the healing of the nations (21:6; 22:1–2)
   v. Babylon's wine which makes the nations drunk (14:8; 17:2; 18:3)

---

[5] Cf. C. Deutsch, 'Transformation of Symbols: The New Jerusalem in Rv 21³–22⁵', *ZNW* 78 (1987), 106–26.

(8) Life and healing (22:1–2)

    v. the blood of slaughter (17:6; 18:24)

(9) God's people are called to enter the New Jerusalem (22:14)

    v. God's people are called to come out of Babylon (18:4).

THE NEW JERUSALEM AS PLACE

The description of the New Jerusalem is a remarkable weaving together of many strands of Old Testament tradition into a coherent and richly evocative image of a place in which people live in the immediate presence of God. It can be considered in its three aspects: place, people, presence of God. We shall study each of these in turn, though without being able to avoid frequent reference to the others.

As a place, the New Jerusalem is at once paradise, holy city and temple. As paradise it is the natural world in its ideal state, rescued from the destroyers of the earth, reconciled with humanity, filled with the presence of God, and mediating the blessings of eschatological life to humanity. As holy city, it fulfils the ideal of the ancient city,[6] as the place where heaven and earth meet at the centre of the earth, from which God rules his land and his people, to whose attraction the nations are drawn for enlightenment, and in which people live in ideal theocentric community. As temple, it is the place of God's immediate presence, where his worshippers see his face.

The 'great high mountain' (21:10) to which the city descends has a long mythological ancestry as well as its immediate derivation from Ezekiel 40:2.[7] It is the cosmic mountain where heaven and earth meet, where the gods dwelt,

---

[6] Cf. J. Dougherty, *The Fivesquare City* (Notre Dame and London: University of Notre Dame Press, 1980), chapter 1.

[7] For the background, see R. J. Clifford, *The Cosmic Mountain in Canaan and the Old Testament* (Cambridge, Mass.: Harvard University Press, 1972); R. L. Cohn, *The Shape of Sacred Space* (AARSR 23; Chico, California: Scholars Press, 1981); F. R. McCurley, *Ancient Myths and Biblical Faith* (Philadelphia: Fortress Press, 1983), part 3; W. J. Dumbrell, *The End of the Beginning: Revelation 21–22 and the Old Testament* (Hombush West, NSW: Lancer Books; Exeter: Paternoster Press, 1985); B. C. Ollenburger, *Zion the City of the Great King* (JSOTSS 41; Sheffield: JSOT Press, 1987).

where sacred cities were built with temples at their heart. Paradise was on 'the holy mountain of God' (Ezek. 28:14). Mount Zion on which Jerusalem and the temple stood was not in reality so very high, but was mythologically a very high mountain (Ezek. 40:2): 'his holy mountain, beautiful in elevation, is the joy of all the earth' (Ps. 48:2). As God's dwelling, the seat of his rule, 'the city of the great King', it was impregnable (Ps. 48). Even if God's throne was in heaven, Mount Zion was his footstool (Ps. 99). In the last days, it was to be elevated above all other mountains, becoming actually the cosmic mountain with which it was symbolically identified, and the temple on its summit would draw all the nations to it (Isa. 2:2). Moreover, it was to be the site of paradise restored (Isa. 11:9; 65:25). Thus the very site of the New Jerusalem in Revelation 21:10 suggests the ideal place. All that the earthly Jerusalem could do no more than symbolize will be reality. Whereas the builders of ancient Babylon (Gen. 11:1–9) sought to join earth to heaven with the self-deifying pride John saw repeated in contemporary Rome, the New Jerusalem which comes from God will truly join heaven to earth.

The New Jerusalem includes paradise in the form of the water of life (22:1–2; cf. 7:17; 21:6; 22:1; 22:17) and the tree of life (22:2; cf. 2:7; 22:14, 19). Both have multiple Old Testament sources which John has himself combined (cf. for the water of life: Isa. 49:10; 55:1; Ezek. 47:1–12; Zech. 14:8; and for the tree of life: Gen. 2:9; 3:24; Ezek. 47:12). Together they represent the food and drink of eschatological life. As the life belonging to the new creation, this is eternal life, unlike the mortal life sustained by the food and drink obtained from this creation. It comes from God (21:6; 22:1), who is himself the life of the new creation, but the imagery suggests that as God's gift of mortal life is mediated to us by this creation of which we are part, so eschatological life will be mediated by the new creation.

Not so obviously, but recognizably to those who were familiar with Jewish traditions, the New Jerusalem is built out of the precious stones and metals of paradise. Havilah, which Jewish interpretation included in paradise, was the source of gold and precious stones (Gen. 2:11–12). Moreover, Ezekiel, in a verse echoed in Revelation 21:19, says to the king of Tyre: 'You were in Eden, the garden of God; every precious stone was your covering' (Ezek. 28:13). The list of every precious stone which follows in the Massoretic text is identical with the first nine of the list of twelve precious stones on the breastplate of the high priest (Exod. 28:17–20), a list of which John also gives a version, as the stones which adorned the twelve foundations of the New Jerusalem (Rev. 21:19–20). From Ezekiel he had learned that this was a list representing all precious stones, all to be found in paradise. Various Jewish traditions claimed that the jewels of the breastplate and other jewels and gold used in the vestments and decoration of the temple came from paradise (the mysterious Parvaim, source of the gold used in Solomon's temple (2 Chron. 3:6; cf. 1QGen.Apoc. 2:23), was identified with paradise). Moreover, an exegetical tradition before Revelation had already identified the precious stones of which the New Jerusalem was to be built, according to Isaiah 54:11–12, with the jewels on the vestments of the high priest, which were supposed to have been so brilliant that they would serve in place of the sun and the moon to light the New Jerusalem (cf. 4QpIsa.ᵃ 1:4–9; L.A.B. 26:13–15). Thus not only the twelve jewels of Revelation 21:19–20, but also the jewels and the gold of which the rest of the city is built (21:18, 21), characterize the New Jerusalem as a temple-city adorned with all the fabulously radiant precious materials of paradise. When the whole city is said to have 'the glory of God and a radiance like a very rare jewel, like jasper, clear as crystal' (21:11), we remember that the glory of God himself is 'like jasper and carnelian' (4:3) and that the sea of glass before his throne in heaven is translucent like crystal, to reflect his glory (4:6). John probably means that the whole city, with its radiant jewels and its translucent gold (21:18, 21), shines with the reflected glory of God himself (cf. 21:23).

The paradisal source of the materials of the New Jerusalem means that they are not to be taken as mere allegories for attributes of the people who inhabit it. The fine linen in which the bride of the Lamb dresses herself, in preparation for her wedding, represents the righteous deeds of the saints (19:7–8), done in this life, but the jewels with which she is decked when her wedding-day comes (21:2, 18–21) are the glory given her by God in the new creation. They are the beauty of the new creation, reflecting the glory of God and made into a home for glorified humanity.

In the beginning God had planted a garden for humanity to live in (Gen. 2:8). In the end he will give them a city. In the New Jerusalem the blessings of paradise will be restored, but the New Jerusalem is more than paradise regained. As a city it fulfils humanity's desire to build out of nature a human place of human culture and community. True, it is given by God and so comes down from heaven. But this does not mean humanity makes no contribution to it. It consummates human history and culture insofar as these have been dedicated to God (cf. 21:12, 14, 24, 26), while excluding the distortions of history and culture into opposition to God that Babylon represents (cf. 21:8, 27; 22:15). It comes from God in the sense that all good comes from God, and all that is humanly good is best when acknowledged to come from God. But the city that both includes paradise unspoiled (22:1–2) and is adorned with the beauty of paradise (21:19) points to that harmony of nature and human culture to which ancient cities once aspired but which modern cities have increasingly betrayed.

As a city, the New Jerusalem is the seat of the divine kingdom. The throne which had been in heaven (chapter 4) is now in the New Jerusalem (22:1, 3). The city is both the light of the world, by which the nations walk (21:24; cf. Isa. 60:3), and the centre to which the nations and their kings come on pilgrimage, bringing tribute (21:24–6; cf. Isa. 60:4–17; Zech. 14:16). But whereas in Isaiah 60:5–17, it is the material wealth of the nations that is brought in tribute to Jerusalem, in Revelation the kings of the earth bring 'their glory' and people bring 'the glory and honour of the nations' (21:26–7). The intention is probably to contrast with Babylon's self-indulgent exploitation of the wealth of her empire at her subject's expense (cf. 18:11–14), as well as to extend the theme of glory that runs through the whole description. In offering their own glory to God's glory, of course the kings and the nations do not lose it, but acknowledge its source in God to whom all glory and honour belong. It is no accident that 'glory and honour' regularly appear in the doxologies of Revelation (4:11; 5:12, 13; 7:12; cf. 19:1).

The description of the New Jerusalem in many respects closely follows Old Testament models (especially Isa. 52:1; 54:11–12; 60; Ezek. 40:2–5; 47:1–12; 48:30–4; Zech. 14:6–21; Tob. 13:16–17). Its most novel feature is the absence of a temple: 'I saw no temple in the city, for its temple is the Lord God Almighty and the Lamb' (21:22). Ezekiel had called the New Jerusalem 'The Lord is There' (Ezek. 48:35), Zechariah had declared the whole city to be as holy as the temple (Zech. 14:20–1), and Isaiah, followed by John (Rev. 21:27), had excluded the ritually unclean from the New Jerusalem, as they were excluded from the temple (Isa. 52:1; Ps. 24:3–4). These prophets had gone far towards envisaging the whole city as the place of God's holy presence, as his truly 'holy mountain'. But John seems to have been the first to eliminate the temple altogether. The city needs no temple, a special place of God's presence, because the whole city is filled with God's immediate presence. As a result the city itself becomes a temple. As well as features already mentioned, the most striking sign of this is its perfectly cubic shape (21:16). In this it is like no city ever imagined, but it is like the holy of holies in the temple (1 Kings 6:20). The radical assimilation of the city to a temple, taken further in Revelation than in its prophetic sources, shows how central to the whole concept of the New Jerusalem in Revelation is the theme of God's immediate presence.

THE NEW JERUSALEM AS PEOPLE[8]

As John sees the New Jerusalem descend from heaven (21:3), he hears its meaning proclaimed:

> Behold, the dwelling of God is with humans.
> He will dwell with them as their God:
> they will be his peoples, and God himself will be with them.
>
> (21:3)

---

[8] For the argument of this section in more detail, see chapter 9 ('The Conversion of the Nations') in Bauckham, *The Climax of Prophecy*.

We have already noticed how these words echo both God's promise to dwell with his own people Israel and to be their God (Ezek. 37:27–8; cf. also Zech. 8:8) and also his promise that many nations will also be his people with whom he will dwell in Zion (Zech. 2:10–11; cf. also Isa. 19:25; 56:7; Amos 9:12). The words are programmatic for the whole account of the New Jerusalem, in the way they combine the language of God's commitment to his covenant people with the most universalistic reference to all people. In saying that 'the dwelling of God is with *humans*' (*meta tōn anthrōpōn*), John uses the word he commonly uses for humanity in general (8:11; 9:6, 10, 15, 18, 20; 13:13; 14:4; 16:8, 9, 21). In saying that 'they will be his *peoples*' (*laoi*), he prefers to the more usual 'nations' (*ethnē*, cf. 2:26; 11:18; 12:5; 14:8; 15:3–4; 18:3, 23; 19:15; 20:3) the plural of the word used for God's covenant people (e.g. Ezek. 37:27). Now that the covenant people have fulfilled their role of being a light to the nations, all nations will share in the privileges and the promises of the covenant people.

Two strands of language and symbolism – referring respectively to the covenant people and to the nations – run through the whole account. In the first place, the history of both Israel and the church comes to fulfilment in the New Jerusalem. The names of the twelve tribes of Israel are on its gates (21:12), as in Ezekiel's vision (Ezek. 48:30–4), while the names of the twelve apostles are on its foundations (21:14). The structures and dimensions of the city are composed of the numbers symbolic of the people of God: twelve (21:12–14, 16, 19–21; cf. 22:2) and 144 (21:17; cf. 7:4; 14:1). It is, after all, the New *Jerusalem*. When the Old Testament covenant formulary ('I will be their God and they will be my people'), which was adapted to apply to all nations in 21:3, is adapted again in 21:7, it forms God's promise to the Christian martyrs, the faithful witnesses whom John's readers are called to become, summing up all the promises made to those who 'conquer' in the seven messages to the churches. Moreover, the climax of the whole account of the New Jerusalem (22:3b–5) portrays the destiny of being 'a kingdom and priests to our God' (5:10; cf. 1:6), which the Lamb won for his Christian followers (5:9; 1:5). In the New

Jerusalem they will worship God in his immediate presence, as priests (22:3b–4), and they will share his reign, as kings (22:5).

On the other hand, the nations walk by the city's light (21:24), the glory and honour of the nations are brought into it (21:26), and the kings of the earth bring their glory into it (21:24). This reference to 'the kings of the earth' is the last occurrence of a phrase which has been used throughout Revelation to refer to the rulers who associate themselves with Babylon and the beast in opposition to God's kingdom (6:15; 17:2, 18; 18:3, 9; 19:19; alluding to Ps. 2:2) and whom Jesus Christ is destined to rule (1:5; cf. 17:14; 19:16). These references to the relationship of nations and kings to the New Jerusalem are based on Isaiah's vision of the New Jerusalem ruling the world (Isa. 60:3, 5, 11). Even more striking is the way that, in Revelation 22:2, John has adapted another Old Testament prophecy to make reference to the nations. The description of the tree of life in 22:2 is based on Ezekiel 47:12, but whereas in Ezekiel the trees bear fruit every month, John has taken this to mean that they bear twelve kinds of fruit, and whereas in Ezekiel the leaves of the trees are simply said to be for healing, John specifies 'the healing of the nations'. Thus, in line with his purpose in the whole description of the New Jerusalem, he combines an allusion to the covenant people (the number twelve) with reference to the nations.

The combination of particularism (reference to the covenant people) and universalism (reference to the nations) in the account of the New Jerusalem could be explained in three ways. In the first place, it has been argued that throughout John intends to refer only to the covenant people redeemed from all the nations (5:9–10). When the rebellious nations have been judged, the covenant people inherit the earth and become the nations and kings of the earth in place of those who once served Babylon and the beast. This explanation fails to take seriously 21:3, in which the overall meaning of the whole account is stated at the outset, as well as the evidence we have studied in our chapter 4 which indicates that in Revelation the witness of the church is intended to bring about the conversion of the nations. Secondly, it might be thought that the covenant people are the inhabitants of the New Jerusalem itself (22:3b–5), while the nations and their kings live outside it and visit it (21:24–6). On this view, the eschatological blessings are shared with the nations, but the covenant people retain a special privilege. But this view also fails to take seriously the implication of 21:3, which declares all the nations to be covenant peoples. If the nations and the kings of the earth have to enter the city by its gates (21:24–6), so do the Christian martyrs (22:14). The image conveys the full inclusion of the nations in the blessings of the covenant, not their partial exclusion. The third explanation is the most probable: that the deliberate mixing of particular and universal imagery throughout the account is a way of maintaining the perspective given in 21:3. It brings together the Old Testament promises for the destiny of God's own people and the universal hope, also to be found in the Old Testament, that all the nations will become God's people. The history of the covenant people – both of the one nation Israel and of the church which is redeemed from all the nations – will find its eschatological fulfilment in the full inclusion of all the nations in its own covenant privileges and promises.

The universalism of the vision of the New Jerusalem completes the direction towards the conversion of the nations which was already clearly indicated in 11:13; 14:14–16; 15:4. Its universal scope should not be minimized. But it should not be taken to mean that Revelation predicts the salvation of each and every human being. Two passages (21:8, 27; cf. 22:15) prevent this conclusion. Unrepentant sinners have no place in the New Jerusalem. The two passages make this point in different, complementary ways. 21:8 is the counterpart to the promise to the one who conquers in 21:7. It warns Christians that if they are not faithful witnesses, but participate in the sins of Babylon, they cannot inherit the holy city, the New Jerusalem, but must suffer the judgment on Babylon's evil (cf. 18:4). (The same combination of promise and warning to Christians recurs in 22:14–15). In 21:8 the imagery used for the fate of sinners is that of divine judgment (cf. 2:11; 14:10; 18:8; 19:20; 20:10, 14–15). In 21:27 the imagery is that of the exclusion of the unholy from the holy presence of God in his holy city (cf. Isa. 52:1). Here those who are threatened with exclusion are those of the nations and their kings (21:24–6) who do not repent (cf. 14:6–11).

THE NEW JERUSALEM AS DIVINE PRESENCE

The theocentricity of Revelation, so apparent in chapters 4–5, is focussed again in the description of the New Jerusalem. God's creation reaches its eschatological fulfilment when it becomes the scene of God's immediate presence. This, in the last resort, is what is 'new' about the new creation. It is the old creation filled with God's presence.

Before chapter 21, Revelation confines the presence of God, as 'the One who sits on the throne', to heaven, where his throne is. This does not mean that he is not now present in the world in any sense, but that his presence is only a paradoxical presence in hiddenness and contradiction. He is present to his worshippers in the sanctuary that is the hidden, inner reality of the persecuted church (11:1–2; cf. 13:6). He is present as the slaughtered Lamb. He is present as the Spirit in the faithful witness of the Lamb's followers who follow him to death. But while the beast rules the world and humanity in general refuses to give God glory, his evident presence, his glory which is inseparable from his reign, appears only in heaven. And when his glory is manifested in heaven, its effect on earth is the destructive judgment of evil (15:7–8). Only when all evil has been destroyed and his kingdom comes, will God's throne be on earth (22:3). Then, when the New Jerusalem comes down from heaven, God will make his home with humanity on earth (21:3). The Greek words which 21:3 uses for 'dwelling' (skēnē) and 'dwell' (skēnoō) are those which Jewish Greek used as virtually transliterations of the Hebrew mishkān and shākan, used in the Old Testament of God's presence in the tabernacle and the temple. Since the whole of the New Jerusalem is a holy of holies, God's immediate presence fills it. In place of a temple, it has the unrestricted presence of God and the Lamb (21:22). Like his presence in the temple (e.g. Ezek. 43), this eschatological presence of God entails holiness and glory. As his eschatological presence, it is also the source of the new life of the new creation.

Holiness we have already mentioned: it is this which excludes the unholy from the holy city (21:27, cf. 2, 10). But the city which is permeated by the divine holiness is also filled with the divine splendour. It needs neither sun nor moon nor lamp (21:23; 22:5), for it has the glory of God (21:11) reflected in the radiance of its own multicoloured translucence (21:11, 18–21). Creation has thus a moral and religious goal – its dedication to God fulfilled in God's holy presence – and also an aesthetic goal – its beauty fulfilled in reflecting the divine glory. The latter is just as theocentric as the former. The new creation, like the old, will have its own God-given beauty, but will be even more beautiful through its evident reflection of God's own splendour. Similarly, the nations and the kings will enjoy their own glory – all the goods of human culture – the more through dedicating it to God's glory. He will be 'all in all' (1 Cor. 15:28), not through the negation of creation, but through the immediacy of his presence to all things.

God's presence, as 'the One who lives for ever and ever' (4:9–10; 10:6; 15:7), also means life in the fullest sense: life beyond the reach of all that now threatens and contradicts life, life which is eternal because it is immediately joined to its eternal source in God. So God gives the water of life (21:6), which flows from his throne (22:1) and waters the tree of life (22:2). All sorrow, suffering and death are banished for ever (21:4). Significantly, this promise is directly linked with God's presence (21:3) by means of the beautiful image John has taken from Isaiah: God himself 'will wipe away every tear from their eyes' (21:4; also 7:17; cf. Isa. 25:8). Whereas God's acts of judgment have been only indirectly attributed to his agency, through intermediaries, here God himself is said to wipe the tears from the faces of all his suffering creatures. The love of God, for which Revelation rarely uses the word 'love' (cf. 1:5; 3:9, 19; 20:9), could hardly be more vividly depicted.

With the final scene around the throne of God and the Lamb (22:3b–5) we are brought back to the central symbol of the whole book: the divine throne, with its combination of cultic and political images, which first appeared in chapters 4–5. We should notice a contrast. In chapters 4–5, in heaven, the living creatures form an inner circle of priests in the immediate presence of God and the twenty-four elders form an inner circle of thrones sharing God's rule. They mediate the worship of the rest of creation. In chapter 22, however, all who may enter the New Jerusalem have immediate access to God's throne on earth. They are priests who worship him and kings who reign with him.

In the earthly temple in Jerusalem the high priest, once a year only, wore the sacred name of God on his forehead and entered God's immediate presence in the holy of holies. In the New Jerusalem, which is God's eternal holy of holies, all will enjoy this immediacy without interruption. But nothing expresses this immediacy more evocatively than the words: 'they shall see his face' (22:4). This is the face of God that no one in mortal life could see and survive (Exod. 33:20–3; Judg. 6:22–3), but to see which is the deepest human religious aspir- ation, to be realized only beyond this mortal life (Ps. 17:15; 1 Cor. 13:12; cf. 4 Ezra 7:98). The face expresses who a person is. To see God's face will be to know who God is in his personal being. This will be the heart of humanity's eternal joy in their eternal worship of God.

As for the image of God's rule in the eschatological kingdom, what is most notable is the fact that all implication of distance between 'the One who sits on the throne' and the world over which he rules has disappeared. His kingdom turns out to be quite unlike the beast's. It finds its fulfilment not in the subject- ion of God's 'servants' (22:3) to his rule, but in their reigning with him (22:5). The point is not that they reign over anyone: the point is that God's rule over them is for them a participa- tion in his rule. The image expresses the eschatological recon- ciliation of God's rule and human freedom, which is also expressed in the paradox that God's service is perfect freedom (cf. 1 Pet. 2:16). Because God's will is the moral truth of our own being as his creatures, we shall find our fulfilment only when, through our free obedience, his will becomes also the spontaneous desire of our hearts. Therefore in the perfection of God's kingdom theonomy (God's rule) and human autonomy (self-determination) will fully coincide. Thus Revelation's final use of its central image of God's throne (22:3b–5) frees it of all the associations of human rule, which must always have subjects, and makes it a pure symbol of the theocentricity of its vision of human fulfilment.

CHAPTER 7

Revelation for today

THE CHRISTIAN CANONICAL PROPHECY

Revelation has a unique place in the Christian canon of Scripture. It is the only work of Christian prophecy that forms part of the canon. Moreover, it is a work of Christian prophecy which understands itself to be the culmination of the whole biblical prophetic tradition. Its continuity with Old Testament prophecy is deliberate and impressively comprehensive. The point may be highlighted by comparing it with the other major work of early Christian prophecy which has survived: the work known as *The Shepherd*, by the Roman Christian prophet Hermas, a work which was popular in the early church, though not finally admitted to the canon. Hermas, despite – or perhaps because of – his Christian prophetic consciousness, virtually ignores the Old Testament. John is steeped in it, not just as the medium in which he thinks, but as the Word of God which he is intepreting afresh for an age in which God's eschatological purpose has begun to be fulfilled. He gathers up all those strands of Old Testament expectation which he understood to point to the eschatological future and focusses them in a fresh vision of the way they are to be fulfilled.

He sees the unity of Old Testament prophecy in its hope for the coming of God's universal kingdom on earth. He reads it in the light of the beginning of the fulfilment of that hope in the life, death and resurrection of Jesus, and in the consequent transformation of the people of God into a people drawn from all nations. He reads the Old Testament in the light of Jesus and his church, but he also interprets Jesus and his church by means of Old Testament prophecy. The latter gives him the expectation that God's universal kingdom must come. His Christian faith gives him the conviction that it is through Jesus' life, death and resurrection that it will come. But he is also a prophet himself, with a fresh revelation to communicate. This is that the church is called to participate in Jesus' victory over evil by following the same path that he trod: the path of faithful witness to the truth even to the point of death. This will be the final conflict of God's people against the powers of this world that oppose God's rule. By this means truth will prevail over the lies by which evil rules. In this way the nations may be won to the worship of the one true God. In this way Jesus will prove to be the one who fulfils all the promises of God. In this way the universal kingdom of God, to which the whole biblical prophetic tradition finally points, will come on earth.

Thus John's own prophetic revelation of the divine purpose, which he claims was revealed to him by Jesus Christ who received it from God, is the focal point around which he is able to draw together a rich variety of images and expectations from the whole prophetic tradition before his time. The process of interpreting Jesus Christ in the light of the Old Testament and the Old Testament in the light of Jesus Christ, which had been going on in the early church from its beginning, and had to go on if the church were not to break Jesus' own complete continuity with the religious tradition of his people, comes to a climax in relation to John's new prophetic revelation. Of course, this is only relatively new. It gives new clarity to those indications in the Old Testament and early Christian tradition which John himself is able to interpret in line with his revelation. Above all, it gives new life to a vision of the future drawn from the prophetic tradition but now envisioned afresh. Small groups of Christians in hostile surroundings, naturally tempted either to assimilate or to turn in on themselves, are challenged to realize that vision by taking on the whole might of the Roman Empire and winning the nations to God by their faithful witness to his truth. From our twentieth-century perspective we need imagination to grasp the full prophetic daring of John's vision.

Given its character and its relation to the rest of the Christian canon of Scripture, the place which Revelation now occupies at the close of the whole canon could not be more appropriate. No other biblical book gathers up so comprehensively the whole biblical tradition in its direction towards the eschatological future. It draws out the sense in which the biblical history, not least its climax in the Christ event, points towards the universal kingdom of God, and it gives the whole canon the character of the book which enables us to live towards that future.

TRUE PROPHECY?

The church's acceptance of Revelation into the New Testament canon was a recognition of it as true prophecy. However, both in the early church and again in the sixteenth century, when questions of canonicity were to some extent reopened, there were those who rejected Revelation. Admittedly, those who doubted its value rarely engaged with more than superficial aspects of the book. But in more recent Christian history a sense that its status as Christian Scripture is problematic has been more widespread. We cannot avoid the question: is it true prophecy? An appropriate response will recognize that this question cannot be answered by the judgment of individuals or groups. It is the use of Scripture as Scripture by the church as a whole over the many centuries of its history in a wide variety of historical contexts which vindicates its capacity to convey the Word of God to God's people. Space precludes a survey of the many ways in which Revelation has been used and misused in the history of the church. But such a survey would show that the popular impression of it as the special preserve of sectarian groups carried away by millenarian fantasy is highly misleading. Of course, there have been and are such groups. But Revelation has persistently inspired the whole church's vision of God and his purpose for history and the eschatological future, perhaps especially in its liturgy, hymns and art.[1] It has

---

[1] For Revelation in art, see M. R. James, *The Apocalypse in Art* (London: Oxford University Press, 1931); F. van der Meer, *Apocalypse: Visions from the Book of Revelation*

been the book both of martyrs[2] and of visionaries: the two groups which have so often saved the church from betraying its witness in compromised conformity to the world. It has been a recurrent source of prophetic critique both of the church itself and of the state and society.[3]

However, it is worthwhile to raise the question of Revelation's status as true prophecy as a way of confronting some of the issues which affect its interpretation as the Word of God for the church today. We may begin by noticing that Revelation's continuity with the Old Testament, which our last section stressed, is precisely what offends some modern critics. Rudolf Bultmann, in a famous phrase, condemned it as 'weakly Christianised Judaism'.[4] But the phrase betrays the influence of the tendency of nineteenth- and early twentieth-century Christianity to deny its Jewish roots. It makes the extraordinary suggestion that only what is not Jewish is really Christian and

---

in Western Art (London: Thames & Hudson, 1978); R. Petraglio *et al.*, *L'Apocalypse de Jean: traditions exégétiques et iconographiques IIIe–XIIIe siècles* (Geneva: Librairie Droz, 1979). Though the text is a somewhat eccentric treatment of Revelation, G. Quispel, *The Secret Book of Revelation* (London: Collins, 1979) is illustrated magnificently with very many examples from the history of western art. Although the influence of Revelation on liturgy and hymns has been considerable, I do not know of any studies. One hymn-writer wrote a devotional commentary on Revelation, interspersed with verse: C. Rossetti, *The Face of the Deep* (London: SPCK, 4th edn, 1902).

[2] See, e.g., W. H. C. Frend, *Martyrdom and Persecution in the Early Church* (Oxford: Blackwell, 1965); R. Bauckham, *Tudor Apocalypse* (Appleford: Sutton Courtenay Press, 1978), especially chapter 2. A commentary on Revelation which applies it to a modern situation of oppression (the suffering of black South Africans under apartheid) is A. A. Boesak, *Comfort and Protest* (Edinburgh: Saint Andrew Press, 1987). Note also the inspiration from Revelation in American black slave spirituals (G. S. Wilmore, *Last Things First* (Philadelphia: Westminster Press, 1972) 77–8) and in the prison meditations of Rumanian pastor Richard Wurmbrand, *Sermons in Solitary Confinement* (London: Hodder & Stoughton, 1969), especially pp. 87, 180.

[3] For the medieval and early modern periods, see M. Reeves, 'The Development of Apocalyptic Thought: Medieval Attitudes'; J. Pelikan, 'Some Uses of the Apocalypse in the Magisterial Reformers'; and B. Capp, 'The Political Dimension of Apocalyptic Thought', all in C. A. Patrides and J. Wittreich, *The Apocalypse in English Renaissance Thought and Literature* (Manchester University Press, 1984), 40–124 (with references to other literature). For a modern example, see Daniel Berrigan, *Beside the Sea of Glass: The Song of the Lamb* (New York: Seabury Press, 1978). See also C. Rowland and M. Corner, *Liberating Exegesis: The Challenge of Liberation Theology to Biblical Studies* (London: SPCK, 1990), chapter 4; O. O'Donovan, 'The Political Thought of the Book of Revelation', *TynB* 37 (1986), 61–94.

[4] R. Bultmann, *Theology of the New Testament*, vol. II, trans. K. Grobel (London: SCM Press, 1955), 175.

that Christianity somehow came into being by negating Judaism. We should now be able to recognize not only the unconscious tendency to anti-Semitism in this approach, but also how aberrant it is, judged by the standard of the whole Christian tradition which consistently claimed the strongest continuity with the Old Testament. It is also historically implausible. As we can now recognize, not only Revelation but all the New Testament documents are the products of a movement best described as a form of first-century Judaism, distinguished from other forms of Judaism not by what it denied in the Jewish religious tradition, but by what it asserted about the way that tradition's hopes for the kingdom of God were being fulfilled by Jesus the Messiah.[5] It was only Christian Gnosticism which tried to deny the continuity. In developing so pervasively the continuity between the faith and hope Christians placed in Jesus and the Old Testament tradition of faith and hope in God, Revelation merely affirms in a rather remarkable way what all early Christians believed. Moreover, it is worth recalling that no other New Testament book can match the astonishing universalism of Revelation's hope for the conversion of the nations and also that this is firmly rooted in the universal hope of the Old Testament prophetic tradition. In becoming a universal religion Christianity did not break but developed its continuity with the Jewish religious tradition.

This means that Revelation's claim to be prophecy must be understood in relation to its claim to continuity with the whole biblical prophetic tradition. It must be understood in terms of the nature of biblical prophecy in general, about which it is worth repeating the platitude that biblical prophecy is much more than prediction. Like biblical prophecy in general, Revelation as prophecy may be said to comprise three closely related elements. First, there is *discernment* of the contemporary situation by prophetic insight into God's nature and purpose. We have noticed Revelation's dominant prophetic concern for

---

[5] Cf. J. D. G. Dunn, *The Partings of the Ways* (London: SCM Press, 1991).

exposing the truth of things – both in the churches and in the world – and for revealing how things look from the perspective of God's heavenly rule. In this way the deceitful ideology of Roman power is exposed and the churches are alerted to the truth of the situation in which they are called to witness. Secondly, there is *prediction*. In John's vision he sees not only 'what is', but also 'what must take place after this' (1:19; cf. 4:1; 1:1). Essentially, the prediction consists in seeing how God's ultimate purpose for the coming of his universal kingdom relates to the contemporary situation as it is perceived by the prophet. What *must* take place is the coming of God's kingdom – or God would not be God. Prophecy as prediction reveals how the contemporary situation must change if God's kingdom is to come. Thirdly, prophecy demands of its hearers an appropriate *response* to its perception of the truth of the contemporary world and its prediction of what the working-out of God's purpose must mean for the contemporary world. It is this third element that ensures that the predictive element in biblical prophecy is not fatalistic. It leaves room for human freedom, for human response to God's will and human participation in his purpose for the world. Jonah's threat of judgment on Nineveh is not fulfilled because Nineveh responds to his prophecy by repenting. God's kingdom must come – or God would not be God – but the predicted manner of its coming is conditional on human response and on God's freedom to embrace human freedom in his purpose. It is true that Jewish apocalyptic tended to a more deterministic view of history than was characteristic of Old Testament prophecy, but we have observed how, in this respect, John is closer to the older prophetic outlook. His prophecy does not predetermine the outcome of the church's calling to witness to the nations. All that is unconditional is that God's kingdom must come and his eschatological renewal of his creation take place. But alongside the hope of the conversion of all the nations to the worship of the true God stands the threat of judgment on the world in its final refusal to acknowledge God's rule.

We have in this book observed several times that Revelation

does not predict a sequence of events, as though it were history written in advance. Such a misunderstanding of the book[6] cannot survive a serious and sensitive study of its imagery. What is specifically predicted as occurring between its own present and the parousia, the final arrival of the kingdom, is a period of conflict between the church and the beast, in which the church will bear its prophetic witness to the nations by persevering in its loyalty to the true God even to the point of death. In this period the powers of evil will do all they can to suppress the church's witness, but their very success in putting Christians to death will be the opportunity for the truth of the church's witness to prove its power to convince and to convert the nations. This 'short' period before the end (cf. 12:12) is symbolized by the apocalyptic period of three and a half years, already a traditional symbol for the period of the final onslaught by the enemies of God against God's people before the End. It ends with the End itself: the coming of Christ to gather the converted nations into his kingdom and to end all opposition to his rule. This is described in a wide range of symbolic images, as is the eschatological consummation of creation in the immediate presence of God which follows.

Thus what John foresees of history before the End itself is that there will be the great conflict, the life-and-death struggle between the beast and the church, in which God's secret strategy for the followers of the Lamb to participate in the coming of God's kingdom is to take effect. Of course, even this is less a prediction than a call to the church to provoke and to win the conflict by persevering in faithful witness. But certainly no sequence of events within this final period of history is predicted. The kaleidoscope of images with which John depicts

---

[6] It is a misunderstanding found both in the 'historicist' tradition of interpretation, which reads Revelation as a symbolic account of the whole history of the church from the time of writing to the parousia (for this tradition in the sixteenth century, see Bauckham, *Tudor Apocalypse*, especially chapter 4; and for a great classic of this tradition, see the four volumes of E. B. Elliott, *Horae Apocalypticae* (London: Seeley, Jackson & Halliday, 5th edn, 1862)), and in the 'futurist' tradition of interpretation, which reads Revelation as a symbolic account of the last few years of history prior to the parousia (for an extraordinarily popular recent version of this tradition, see Hal Lindsey, *The Late Great Planet Earth* (London: Lakeland, 1971), and the critique in C. Vanderwaal, *Hal Lindsey and Biblical Prophecy* (Ontario: Paideia, 1978)).

it are concerned with its nature and meaning. They explore the character of the beast's power and deceit, the ineffectiveness of mere judgments to bring about repentance, the power of suffering witness to convince of truth, the relationship of the church's witness to that of Jesus, and so on. Above all, they give the church the heavenly perspective on the meaning of the conflict and the nature of victory in it that the church will need in order to persevere in its costly witness throughout.

To anyone who accepts the perceptive element in John's prophecy it is obvious in what a remarkable sense the predictive element proved true in the two centuries after it was written. By the end of the period of the persecutions, on the eve of the Constantinian revolution which dramatically changed the church's relation to the Empire, Christians, though still a minority, had become a sizeable minority to be reckoned with. Persecution for much of the period was local and sporadic, but in the third century the growth of Christianity provoked the series of great persecutions which were determined attempts to stamp it out. Christianity was not perceived as just another degenerate eastern cult, but as in conflict with the whole pagan view of the world and in particular with the absolutist claims of the Roman imperial ideology. Throughout the period martyrdom played a major role in the success of the Christian Gospel. Of course, the historical evidence is not available to weigh it against other factors. But it is clear that not only was martyrdom frequently the way in which the claims of the Christian God were brought to inescapable public attention, but also that the fact of the martyrs' willingness to die and the way in which they died were seen to cohere with the nature of the religious message they believed. Moreover, John's own prophecy played a role, as it was intended to do, in providing the church with the vision that made martyrdom possible and meaningful.[7]

The nature of Christianity's eventual historical victory over the pagan Empire is, of course, far more ambivalent. In the

---

[7] Note, e.g., the allusions to Revelation in the Letter of the Churches of Lyons and Vienne (ap. Eusebius, *Hist. Eccl.* 5.1.1–5.4.3), one of the earliest accounts of martyrdoms – especially the allusions to Rev. 14:4 (5.1.10) and Rev. 1:5; 3:14 (5.2.3).

Christian empire and its successors the beast constantly reappeared in ever new Christian disguises. The reader of Revelation need not be surprised, since the beast and Babylon have their counterparts and agents already within the seven churches of Asia. But clearly the conversion of the Empire was not the coming of the eschatological kingdom. History, with all its ambivalence as the scene of struggle between truth and deceit, in which God's kingdom is present only in hiddenness and contradiction and the devil's power to deceive the nations with the idolatries of power and prosperity is by no means abolished, continued and continues. Moreover, the history we have sketched is a small, though significant, part of world history. Even for John, who must have known of many nations, not only the Parthians, far beyond the boundaries of the Empire, the statements that the beast rules all the nations of the world (13:7–8) and that all nations have drunk Babylon's wine (14:8; 18:3, cf. 23–34; cf. 17:18) must have been deliberately hyperbolic, but for us they seem very much more so. The church's struggle with the Roman Empire not only was not, but could not have been the last stage, short of the parousia, in the achievement of God's universal kingdom on earth.

Thus John's prophecy was remarkably fulfilled, but not by the coming of the kingdom. It retains, as it were, an unfulfilled, eschatological excess. Here it is important to revert to the nature of biblical prophecy in general. Biblical prophecy always *both* addressed the prophet's contemporaries about their own present and the future immediately impending for them *and* raised hopes which proved able to transcend their immediate relevance to the prophet's contemporaries and to continue to direct later readers to God's purpose for their future. Historicizing modern scholarship has sometimes stressed the former to the total exclusion of the latter, forgetting that most biblical prophecy was only preserved in the canon of Scripture because its relevance was not exhausted by its reference to its original context. Conversely, fundamentalist interpretation, which finds in biblical prophecy coded predictions of specific events many centuries later than the prophet, misunderstands prophecy's continuing relevance by neglecting to ask what it meant to its first hearers. It is important, as we have done in this book, to understand how John's prophecy addressed his contemporaries, since they are the only readers it explicitly addresses. This does not prevent us from appreciating but helps us to understand how it may also transcend its original context and speak to us.

Two features of the way biblical prophecy proved to have continuing relevance to later readers are relevant. In the first place, in the biblical tradition God's purposes in history were understood to be consistent, and therefore his great acts of salvation and judgment in the past could be understood as models for what he would do in the future. This is why, for example, the imagery of the exodus came to play so important a part, not least in Revelation, in depicting the eschatological events of salvation and judgment. But it also meant that prophecies which had been fulfilled could be reinterpreted and reapplied to new situations. When John echoed the Old Testament prophecies of the doom of Babylon and the doom of Tyre, using them to compose his own prophecy of the fall of Babylon, he was not ignorant of their original reference to the great pagan powers contemporary with the prophets who pronounced those oracles. But he saw Rome as the successor to Tyre in its economic empire and the successor to Babylon in its political oppression. Since the evil of these cities was echoed and surpassed by Rome, how much more must God's judgment on them fall also on Rome. The city which the prophetic cap fits must wear it. Such a principle allows prophetic oracles to transcend their original reference, without supposing that somehow when Jeremiah referred to Babylon he really meant Rome. The same principle validates the way in which Revelation has inspired prophetic critiques of later systems of political and economic oppression throughout the church's history and still does so today.

Secondly, prophetic promise frequently exceeded fulfilment. For example, the restoration of Israel after the Babylonian exile did not match up to the terms in which the great prophets of the exile foresaw it. In one sense their prophecies were vindicated, but in another sense they continued to inspire hopes for a much greater salvation event in which God would be vindicated universally as the God both of his people and of the nations of the world. In this excess of promise over fulfilment lay the roots of much apocalyptic eschatology. John's own vision of the New Jerusalem has developed from the visions of the prophets of the exile which the actual rebuilding of Jerusalem and the temple after the exile fell far short of realizing. There is a sense in which much of the biblical prophetic tradition has an eschatological tendency. That is, the contemporary situation is brought into direct relationship with a final resolution of history in the coming of God's kingdom. Isaiah already envisages the paradisal rule of universal peace and justice by the messianic shoot from the stump of Jesse as the critique and imminent replacement of the militaristic oppression of the Assyrian empire, just as John expects the victory of the martyrs and God's judgment of the Roman system of power to mean the arrival of the universal kingdom of God at the parousia of Jesus Christ. In the later prophets and the apocalyptic tradition this eschatological tendency only becomes more explicit and defined. It seems to be intrinsic to the biblical prophetic tradition of perceiving God's will for the immediate situation in terms of his ultimate purposes of righteousness and grace for his whole creation. That it was a non-problematic feature of the tradition is shown by the way such prophecy was not rejected as false but taken up into the tradition of Jewish and Christian hope. Fulfilments of prophecy were real and recognized, but fell short of the eschatological excess of expectation which the prophecies raised and which could be satisfied only by God's final victory over all evil. The delay of this final victory was problematic for the same reason that the problem of evil itself is necessarily problematic for all theistic believers. But the prophecies themselves were evidently not problematic. Their provisional fulfilments, within the ambiguities of history, sustained hope for the coming of the eschatological kingdom itself.

There is a sense in which Revelation, as the culmination of the biblical prophetic tradition, is peculiarly able to transcend its original context of relevance. It gathers up and re-envisions many of the strands of biblical prophecy which had most clearly surpassed their own original contexts and inspired the continuing hopes of God's people. Moreover, in doing so it combines a contextual specificity of relevance to its first readers with a kind of eschatological hyperbole that intrinsically transcends their context. As we have already observed, it constantly uses emphatically universal language both about the power and dominion and worship of the beast and about the mission and witness of the church. The church is drawn from every nation (5:9) and constitutes an innumerable multitude (7:9). Its witness, symbolized by the angel's proclamation of the eternal gospel, goes out to all nations (14:6). The expected period of trial under the rule of the beast is coming on the whole world (3:10). The beast has authority over every nation and is worshipped by all the inhabitants of the earth (13:7–8). The second beast enforces his worship by a system of totalitarian control of economic life (13:12–17) which, though it fulfils the logic of the beast's kind of power, far exceeds not merely the realities, but the possibilities of the first century. The dragon, the beast and the false prophet assemble the kings of the whole world for the final battle at Armageddon (16:14). Babylon deceives all the nations (14:8; 18:3, 23) and is guilty of the blood of all who have been slaughtered on earth (18:24). Even allowing for the limitations of the geographical horizon of first-century people, all this must be deliberately hyperbolic. It depicts the impending conflict between the church and the beast in terms which are eschatologically universal rather than historically realistic. It superimposes the vision of the coming of God's universal kingdom on the immediate future which John and his readers confront.

This does not mean that John predicts, in some distant future, centuries later than the Roman Empire, a truly universal, totalitarian, anti-Christian state. The hyperbole is of the same kind as another we have noticed in chapter 4 above: the way John writes *as though* all Christians are to suffer martyrdom. The hyperbole makes clear what is at stake in the conflict between the church and the Empire. That conflict truly concerns the coming of God's universal kingdom. But the hyperbole also shows that what is at stake in the conflict of that time is what is always at stake in the church's history. The beast as the Roman Empire never held truly universal power, but what the beast represents, in a thousand other historical forms, contests the control of God's world until the coming of his eschatological kingdom. Therefore also the street of the great city, in which the witnesses to God's truth lie dead at the hands of the beast, need be neither in Jerusalem nor in Rome nor even in the cities of Asia. It may also be wherever the unprecedented numbers of Christian martyrs in our own century have died. The eschatological hyperbole gives these symbols intrinsic power to reach as far as the parousia. Furthermore, it is not only the hyperbole that gives the images this power. Because John's images are images designed to penetrate the essential character of the forces at work in his contemporary world and the ultimate issues at stake in it, to a remarkable extent they leave aside the merely incidental historical features of his world. There are enough of them to make the reference unmistakable: Babylon is built on seven hills (17:9) and trades in a very accurate list of the imports to first-century Rome from all over the known world (18:11–13).[8] But they are sufficiently few to make the reapplication of the images to comparable situations easy. Any society whom Babylon's cap fits must wear it. Any society which absolutizes its own economic prosperity at the expense of others comes under Babylon's condemnation.

Thus Revelation, in its predictive element, found fulfilment in its own immediate future and also finds a continuing relevance that transcends its original context and may still inspire and inform hope for the coming of God's kingdom. In this combination of fulfilment and eschatological excess, John's prophecy proves true to the tradition of biblical prophecy, and for those who find that tradition's vision of the world convincing it proves true.

---

[8] R. Bauckham, 'The Economic Critique of Rome in Revelation 18', in L. Alexander ed., *Images of Empire* (*JSO*TSS 122; Sheffield: *JSOT* Press, 1991), 58–79, which is chapter 10 in Bauckham, *The Climax of Prophecy*.

IMMINENCE AND DELAY

The same issue which we have discussed in the last section has a
further aspect which is worth noticing, if only because modern
readers frequently find it problematic. This is the imminent
expectation, which Revelation shares with most of the New
Testament documents. John's prophecy is a revelation of 'what
must *soon* take place' (1:1; cf. 1:3; 22:10: 'the time is near').
This cannot mean only that the great conflict of the church and
the Empire is soon to *begin*, for the parousia itself is also said to
be soon. Three times in the epilogue, Jesus himself promises, 'I
am coming soon' (22:7, 12, 20; cf. 2:16; 3:11). Many have
thought early Christianity's eschatological expectation itself to
be invalidated by this sense of temporal imminence. Such a
conclusion renders much of the New Testament problematic,
but none more so than this book which is so dominated by the
eschatological expectation.

However, eschatological delay is as much a feature of Revelation as eschatological imminence. It is written into the
structure of the book. From the moment the martyrs cry, 'How
long?' and are told to wait a little while longer (6:10–11), the
reader – and more especially, the hearer of an oral performance of Revelation – becomes conscious of the tension of
imminence and delay, as the End is constantly approached but
not definitively reached. Disappointingly moderate series of
warning judgments progress rather slowly towards the
expected climax in the final judgment. The interludes between
the sixth and seventh seal-openings and between the sixth and
seventh trumpet-blasts both symbolize and explain the delay.
In the crucial chapters 10–11, we learn that there is to be no
more delay for the sake of further warning judgments (10:3–6)
and that there is to be a delay, lasting the symbolic period of
three-and-a-half years (11:3), for the sake of the church's
prophetic witness to the world. John here creates his own
version of the tension between eschatological imminence and
eschatological delay that runs through the whole apocalyptic
tradition. The logic of imminence is that God's kingdom must
come. Evil is triumphant and the righteous suffer: surely this

contradiction to God's purpose cannot continue indefinitely? If God is the righteous God he must soon put all wrongs to right. But the logic of delay is that of God's patience and grace. He gives people time to repent. John's revelation of the role of the church's suffering witness deepens this logic. That very suffering of the righteous which, for the apocalyptic tradition, demands God's imminent intervention to establish his kingdom, is actually God's strategy for establishing his kingdom.

The three-and-a-half year period is, of course, symbolic. (Anyone who doubts that Revelation's time-periods are all symbolic should consider 2:10; 17:12.) It is also characterized as 'a little while' (6:11; 12:12; 17:10), a phrase which, like the period of three and a half years, has an exegetical basis and a traditional role in consideration of the eschatological delay (Ps. 37:10; Isa. 26:20; Heb. 10:37). It assures the church that her time of trial is not indefinite. In God's purpose it has a limit and the kingdom will finally come. It is consistent with Jesus' promise to come 'soon', but in a way that removes the possibility of chronological calculation. The church which prays for the coming of the kingdom and hopes for the conversion of the nations lives in the tension of imminence and delay. That the tension is theological rather than merely chronological explains why the delay of the parousia was not the kind of problem for the early church that it became for modern New Testament scholars.[9]

The really important effect of the imminent expectation in Revelation is that it enables John to bring his prophetic vision of the final outcome of history to bear on his understanding of the contemporary situation. It is as he sees God's purpose of finally establishing his universal kingdom impinging on the present that John is able to perceive God's purpose in the present situation and the role that Christians are called to play in that purpose with a view to the coming of the kingdom. In this prophetic process of confronting the present with God's final purpose for history there is the implicit recognition that

[9] See further R. Bauckham, 'The Delay of the Parousia', *TynB* 31 (1980), 3–36.

the End of history bears a unique relationship to the whole of history. It is not just the last thing to happen, coming after the penultimate historical event. It is the point at which the truth of all history comes to light. It is the divine judgment on the value and meaning of all history. In that sense, the imminent expectation of the early Christians was a way of living in the light of what history is finally, in God's purpose, all about. It sees every moment of life in relation to the coming of God's kingdom. We cannot artificially reproduce this sense of imminence in the temporal form it took for many earlier generations of Christians. But we need a kind of second naivety in which, beyond the superficial obstacle of the delay of the parousia, we can share the early Christian sense of the relation of meaning between the present and the eschatological kingdom of God.

REVELATION'S RELEVANCE TODAY

This final section is far from exhaustive. It does not attempt to pre-empt the ways in which readers may find their own routes from engaging with Revelation's theology to contextualizing it in a contemporary situation. It merely highlights briefly some points which have emerged in this study as offering theological directions for contemporary reflection:

(1) We have suggested that one of the functions of Revelation was to purge and to refurbish the Christian imagination. It tackles people's imaginative response to the world, which is at least as deep and influential as their intellectual convictions. It recognizes the way a dominant culture, with its images and ideals, constructs the world for us, so that we perceive and respond to the world in its terms. Moreover, it unmasks this dominant construction of the world as an ideology of the powerful which serves to maintain their power. In its place, Revelation offers a different way of perceiving the world which leads people to resist and to challenge the effects of the dominant ideology. Moreover, since this different way of perceiving the world is fundamentally to open it to transcendence it resists any absolutizing of power or structures or ideals within this

world. This is the most fundamental way in which the church is called always to be counter-cultural. The necessary purging and refurbishing of the Christian imagination must, of course, always be as contextual as Revelation was in its original context, but Revelation can help to inform and to inspire it.

(2) It needs to be added at once that Revelation is overwhelmingly concerned with the *truth* of God. So we should not construe the notion of different imaginative ways of perceiving the world in the vulgarly postmodern way that reduces all significant truth to matters of personal preference and ends in nihilism. Revelation gives us no warrant for mistaking images for truth itself, but it seeks images that conform to truth and seeks to use images in a way that conforms to truth. It reminds us that the church's witness to the world is authentic only as primarily a witness to truth – to the one true God and the truth of his righteousness and grace. In western societies today this witness to the truth does not confront a totalitarian ideology which claims sole truth and seeks to suppress the Gospel. Instead it faces a relativistic despair of the possibility of truth and, even more, a consumerist neglect of the relevance of truth. The church's witness will be of value only if it knows truth worth dying for.

(3) The alternative vision of the world which Revelation claims to be orientated to the truth is strongly theocentric. In this it shows the power of a theocentric vision to confront oppression, injustice and inhumanity. In the end it is only a purified vision of the transcendence of God that can effectively resist the human tendency to idolatry which consists in absolutizing aspects of this world. The worship of the true God is the power of resistance to the deification of military and political power (the beast) and economic prosperity (Babylon). In the modern age we may add that it is what can prevent movements of resistance to injustice and oppression from dangerously absolutizing themselves.

(4) Revelation resists the dominant ideology not only by its reference to the transcendent God (heaven) but also by its reference to an alternative future (the new creation and the New Jerusalem). By seeing the world as open to divine tran-

scendence it opens the world to the coming of God's kingdom. It is this which makes possible both the full recognition of injustice and oppression and the relativizing of the structures, however powerful, which presently maintain them.

(5) As well as Revelation's perspective from above (the divine transcendence in heaven) and from the eschatological future, it also in some sense adopts a perspective from below, that is, from the standpoint of the victims of history. This is a standpoint taken in solidarity, rather than necessarily where John and his readers are by social and economic status. But it is the result of standing for God and his kingdom against the idolatries of the powerful. Insofar as Revelation's theology might be called a liberation theology, it speaks to the affluent and the powerful as much as to the poor and oppressed.

(6) Revelation does not respond to the dominant ideology by promoting Christian withdrawal into a sectarian enclave that leaves the world to its judgment while consoling itself with millennial dreams. Since this is the standard caricature of the apocalyptic mentality, it must be strongly emphasized that it is the opposite of Revelation's outlook, which is orientated to the coming of God's kingdom in the whole world and calls Christians to active participation in this coming of the kingdom. In its daring hope for the conversion of all the nations to the worship of the true God it develops the most universalistic features of the biblical prophetic tradition. In its conception of the church's prophetic witness as standing for the true God and his righteousness against the political and economic idolatries of Rome it is faithful to the prophetic tradition's conviction that the true worship of the true God is inseparable from justice and truth in all aspects of life. It is in the public, political world that Christians are to witness for the sake of God's kingdom. Worship, which is so prominent in the theocentric vision of Revelation, has nothing to do with pietistic retreat from the public world. It is the source of resistance to the idolatries of the public world. It points representatively to the acknowledgment of the true God by all the nations, in the universal worship for which the whole creation is destined.

(7) It is Revelation's orientation towards God's universal kingdom which accounts for its emphasis on future eschatology. The critics, already mentioned, who see Revelation as an insufficiently Christianized form of Judaism, often have this in mind, contrasting Revelation with the greater emphasis on realized eschatology in some other New Testament writings. But merely to contrast relative emphases is to miss the point. In the theology of Revelation it is foundational that the eschatological victory of Jesus Christ has already been won, and its immediate result, in constituting a people of God drawn from all nations, is a kind of realization of God's kingdom in the sense that this people already acknowledges God's rule. The emphasis on future eschatology comes from the recognition that this is not the goal of God's purpose. The sense in which God's kingdom has not yet come is that the powers which dominate the world do so in defiance of God and his righteousness. The church does not exist for itself, but in order to participate in the coming of God's universal kingdom. The victory the Messiah has already won is the decisive eschatological event, but it cannot have reached its goal until all evil is abolished from God's world and all the nations are gathered into the Messiah's kingdom. This is indeed a Jewish apocalyptic perspective on the Christian salvation-event, but it is an entirely necessary counterweight to a kind of realized eschatology which so spiritualizes the kingdom of God as to forget the unredeemed nature of the world. Revelation's future eschatology serves to keep the church orientated towards God's world and God's future for the world.

(8) Revelation's prophetic critique is of the churches as much as of the world. It recognizes that there is a false religion not only in the blatant idolatries of power and prosperity, but also in the constant danger that true religion falsify itself in compromise with such idolatries and betrayal of the truth of God. Again, this is the relevance of Revelation's theocentric emphasis on worship and truth. The truth of God is known in genuine worship of God. To resist idolatry in the world by faithful witness to the truth, the church must continuously purify its own perception of truth by the vision of the utterly

Holy One, the sovereign Creator, who shares his throne with the slaughtered Lamb.

(9) Christian participation in God's purpose of establishing his kingdom is portrayed in Revelation as a matter of witness, primarily verbal, but substantiated by life. It should not surprise us that possibilities of changing society by the use of power and influence in accordance with the values of God's kingdom are not envisaged. It is doubtful whether this should be attributed to the apocalyptic perception of the world, as it often is, as though it would otherwise have been possible to see things differently. This feature of the so-called apocalyptic perception of the world corresponded to the realistic situation of Christians in the first-century Roman Empire and for that reason persists in Revelation, which otherwise modifies the apocalyptic perception of the world in many ways, including the idea of the church's witness to the world. Of course, in other situations, different possibilities of serving God's kingdom in the world open up. They do so as a quite natural extension of Revelation's concept of witness as involving obedience to God's commandments, that is, embodying his kingdom in life. But Revelation's reminder that Christian participation in the coming of God's kingdom is not dependent on power and influence remains important. The essential form of Christian witness, which cannot be replaced by any other, is consistent loyalty to God's kingdom. In this powerless witness the power of truth to defeat lies comes into its own. Legitimate power and influence are certainly not to be despised, but the temptations of power are best resisted when the priority of faithful witness is maintained.

(10) In Revelation's universal perspective, the doctrines of creation, redemption and eschatology are very closely linked. It is God the Creator of all reality who, in faithfulness to his creation, acts in Christ to reclaim and renew his whole creation. Because he is creation's Alpha he will also be its Omega. The scope of his new creation is as universal as the scope of creation. It is as Creator that he claims his universal kingdom. It is as Creator that he can renew his creation, taking it beyond the threat of evil and nothingness into the eternity of his own presence. An important contribution of Revelation to New

Testament theology is that it puts the New Testament's central theme of salvation in Christ clearly into its total biblical–theological context of the Creator's purpose for his whole creation. This is a perspective that needs recovering today.

(11) Throughout this study we have stressed not only Revelation's theocentricity, which means that all other aspects of its vision of the world stem from its understanding of God, but also that this understanding of God is itself a sophisticated product of serious theological reflection. Sadly, this doctrine of God has been the most misunderstood feature of a much misunderstood book. Revelation has the most developed trinitarian theology in the New Testament, with the possible exception of the Gospel of John, and is all the more valuable for demonstrating the development of trinitarianism quite independently of hellenistic philosophical categories. It has a powerful, apophatic perception of the transcendence of God which entirely avoids and surmounts current criticism of monarchical images of transcendence. At the same time as it withholds the glory of God from a world in which the powers of evil still hold sway, it recognizes the presence of God in this present world in the form of the slaughtered Lamb and the seven Spirits who inspire the church's witness. By placing the Lamb on the throne and the seven Spirits before the throne it gives sacrificial love and witness to truth the priority in the coming of God's kingdom in the world, while at the same time the openness of the creation to the divine transcendence guarantees the coming of the kingdom. God's rule does not contradict human freedom, as the coercive tyranny of the beast does, but finds its fulfilment in the participation of people in God's rule: that is, in the coincidence of theonomy and autonomy. Finally, the divine transcendence does not prevent but makes possible the eschatological destiny of creation to exist in immediate relation to God, his immanent presence its glory and its eternal life. This recapitulation of the main points in the understanding of God which has been expounded throughout this study are intended to suggest that Revelation has an unexpected theological relevance today: it can help to inspire the renewal of the doctrine of God which is perhaps the most urgent contemporary theological need.

Further reading

The following books and articles are some of the more useful for studying specifically the theology of Revelation.

Barr, D. L. 'The Apocalypse as a Symbolic Transformation of the World: A Literary Analysis', *Int.* 38 (1984), 39–50.
'The Apocalypse of John as Oral Enactment', *Int.* 40 (1986), 243–56.
Bauckham, R. *The Climax of Prophecy: Studies on the Book of Revelation.* Edinburgh: T. & T. Clark, 1992. A collection of essays, many of which develop aspects of the argument of the present book at greater length.
Beasley-Murray, G. R. *The Book of Revelation.* NCB. London: Marshall, Morgan & Scott, 1974. A reliable commentary which is alert to theological issues.
Boring, M. E. 'The Theology of Revelation: "The Lord Our God the Almighty Reigns"', *Int.* 40 (1986), 257–69.
Bovon, F. 'Le Christ de L'Apocalypse', *RTP* 21 (1972), 65–80.
Caird, G. B. *A Commentary on the Revelation of St John the Divine.* BNTC. London: A & C. Black, 1966. A commentary notable for its attempt to read Revelation as a thoroughly Christian reinterpretation of Old Testament images and themes.
Comblin, J. *Le Christ dans l'Apocalypse.* Bibliothèque de Théologie: Théologie biblique 3/6. Paris: Desclée, 1976. This major study of the Christology (and related themes) of Revelation was written independently of that of Holtz (see next item). An appended note (pp. 237–40) points out Comblin's differences from Holtz.
Holtz, T. *Die Christologie der Apokalypse des Johannes.* TU 85. Berlin: Akademie Verlag, 1962. The standard, very thorough study of its subject, which nevertheless can be usefully complemented by Comblin's rather different approach (see preceding item).
'Gott in der Apokalypse', in J. Lambrecht, ed., *L'Apocalyptique johannique et l'Apocalyptique dans le Nouveau Testament.* BETL 53; Gembloux: Duculot and Leuven: University Press, 1980, 247–65.

Mazzaferri, F. D. *The Genre of the Book of Revelation from a Source-Critical Perspective.* BZNW 54. Berlin and New York: de Gruyter, 1989. Though primarily concerned with arguing that Revelation belongs to the literary genre of prophecy, this study is broader than its title suggests and has much insight into many issues of interpretation.

Minear, P. S. 'Ontology and Ecclesiology in the Apocalypse', *NTS* 12 (1966), 89–105.

I Saw a New Earth: An Introduction to the Visions of the Apocalypse. Washington and Cleveland: Corpus, 1968. Though Minear's thesis that Revelation is not a critique of the Roman Empire but solely of the church fails finally to convince, this is a book packed with fresh and sensitive insight.

Rissi, M. *Time and History: A Study of the Revelation.* Trans. G. C. Winsor. Richmond, Virginia: John Knox Press, 1966. This is an attempt to fit Revelation into a *heilsgeschichtliche* (salvation-historical) theological framework.

Schüssler Fiorenza, E. *The Book of Revelation: Justice and Judgment.* Philadelphia: Fortress, 1985. A collection of major essays by one of the foremost American experts on Revelation.

Sweet, J. P. M. *Revelation.* SCM Pelican Commentaries. London: SCM Press, 1979. Sweet's interpretation is in the tradition of G. B. Caird and Austin Farrer (whose best insights he extracts from the more eccentric), and is notably alert to the significance of Old Testament allusions and the range of associations of the imagery. Probably the best short English commentary.

'Maintaining the Testimony of Jesus: the Suffering of Christians in the Revelation of John', in W. Horbury and B. McNeil, ed., *Suffering and Martyrdom in the New Testament: Studies presented to G. M. Styler.* Cambridge University Press, 1981, 101–17.

Trites, A. A. *The New Testament Concept of Witness.* SNTSMS 31. Cambridge University Press, 1977. Chapter 10. The most important study of this theme in Revelation.

Vögtle, A. 'Der Gott der Apokalypse: Wie redet die christliche Apokalypse von Gott', in J. Coppens, ed., *La Notion biblique de Dieu: Le Dieu de la Bible et le Dieu des philosophes.* BETL 41; Gembloux: Duculot and Leuven: University Press, 1976, 377–98.

Yarbro Collins, A. *Crisis and Catharsis: The Power of the Apocalypse.* Philadelphia: Westminster Press, 1984. An attempt to understand the message of the book in sociological and psychological terms.

Index